Frederico Fernandez Cavada

Libby Life

Experiences of a Prisoner of War in Richmond, 1863-64

Frederico Fernandez Cavada

Libby Life
Experiences of a Prisoner of War in Richmond, 1863-64

ISBN/EAN: 9783744761345

Printed in Europe, USA, Canada, Australia, Japan

Cover: Foto ©ninafisch / pixelio.de

More available books at **www.hansebooks.com**

LIBBY LIFE:

EXPERIENCES

OF

A PRISONER OF WAR

IN RICHMOND, VA., 1863-64,

BY

LIEUT. COLONEL F. F. CAVADA,

U. S. V.

PHILADELPHIA:
KING & BAIRD, 607 SANSOM STREET.
1864.

Entered according to Act of Congress, in the year 1864, by

ROBERT P. KING,

In the Clerk's Office of the District Court in and for the Eastern District of Pennsylvania.

PRINTED BY KING & BAIRD.

TO

The Union League of Philadelphia,

THIS BOOK

AN HUMBLE TOKEN OF SYMPATHY WITH THEIR
PATRIOTIC EFFORTS,

IS

MOST RESPECTFULLY DEDICATED.

CONTENTS.

INTRODUCTORY.

I.

1863. July:—The Libby Prison—Early Experiences—A Rainy Day—Our Commissariat—Unpleasant Reflections—Scrubbing Day, and White-washing Day—The Lyceum, and the Libby Chronicle—A Lecture on Mesmerism and its consequences. 21

II.

August:—Killing Time—The New Arrival—Experiences of a "Fresh Fish"—Episodes of Daily Life—A Prayer—Starvation—About a Tub—A Mock Trial. . . . 39

III.

September:—Amatory—The Catechism—Nocturnal Sports—The Fate of a Union Officer, charged with being a Spy—Distribution of Rooms. 59

IV.

October:—Preparing for Winter—Sports—The Elections—A Yankee Trick. 71

V.

NOVEMBER:—Various Forms of Melancholy—Confederate Wails—Surgeons and Chaplains—Supplies from the North—The Great Conspiracy. 81

VI.

DECEMBER:—Shadows—Musical—Christmas—New Year's Eve—A Story about Six Eggs—Another Story. 93

VII.

1864. JANUARY:—New Year's Day—Speculative and Retrospective—Lugubrious—Escapes from the Prison—Belle Isle. 123

VIII.

FEBRUARY:—A Sermon from a Candle—The Prison World—Crowded Condition of the Prison—Cooking Experiences—Letters—The Grand Escapade. 147

IX.

MARCH:—Reveries—Matter of Fact—Matrimonial—Consolatory—Rumors—Huckster Officers—Confederate Currency and Prices—"Tunnel on the Brain"—A Search—Boxes—Gen. Kilpatrick's Raid—The Gunpowder Plot—Paroled—Conclusion. 177

APPENDIX. 201

PREFACE.

THE following notes were written, and the sketches which illustrate them were drawn, not with the object of presenting a sensational picture of the military prisons of the Confederacy, but simply to while away the idle hours of a tedious and protracted captivity. Such scenes were therefore preferred as, owing to their entertaining character, were best calculated to dispel the gloom of the prison, and those were treated as briefly as possible, which would have only added to that gloom, by a prolonged contemplation of their miseries. A journal, or connected narrative, would have proved too monotonous; I have endeavored, however, so to arrange the order of events described, as to preserve a sufficient degree of chronological consistency. My chief aim in these humble pages has been to perpetuate for my companions in captivity, a compliance with their request, a truthful record of our prison experiences,—a record which, while it cannot fail to bring back upon our hearts some of the gloomy shadows which once darkened them in the prison-house, may also renew upon our lips the irrepressible smiles which were wont to wreathe them at times, in spite of hunger, suffering and despair.

F. F. C.

CONTINENTAL HOTEL, PHILADELPHIA,
May, 1864.

INTRODUCTORY.

INTRODUCTORY.

EARLY in the morning of the 3d of July, 1863. a long, straggling column of Federal prisoners, captured during the preceding day on the battle-field of Gettysburg, was marching on the Chambersburg road to the rear of the Rebel lines. With the gray dawn we had seen General Lee and his staff making their way to the front; and soon after, the fearful cannonading commenced which opened the contest of that memorable day. On reaching Willoughby creek we were halted, and lay down to rest in the woods. We were only three miles from the field of battle, and the incessant reverberations of the artillery, and the rapid discharges of musketry, reached our ears with a continuous roar, which told how bloody was the struggle, and how well disputed the ground. The following day we heard rumors of the repulse and defeat of the Rebels, and unmistakable indications soon led us to believe that our captors were in full retreat.

On that 4th of July, so glorious for our arms, our column was once more started, drenched with the torrents of rain which fell without intermission. The Rebel trains and artillery were moving rapidly in the direction of Chambersburg. Before we had proceeded far we were joined by the prisoners captured during the engagement of the 1st, making an aggregate of about two thousand. We were marched steadily over the rough mountain roads until after midnight, having proceeded as far as Monterey Springs. It would be difficult to give a description which could do justice to the trials of that weary night-march; we were pressed forward at the utmost speed of which we were capable, and many, unable to keep up with the column, fell exhausted by the road side. Along with us were long trains of wagons, and a motley assortment of vehicles of all kinds, impressed from the farmers of the neighborhood, loaded with the Rebel wounded.

The next morning, before we had time to partake of a generous breakfast prepared for us by some of the inhabitants of the place, we were again ordered into line, and resumed our march towards Hagerstown. We had proceeded but a short distance when we heard rapid firing in our rear, and we flattered ourselves with the hope that we might yet be rescued. The cannonading, we ascertained, was by the artillery of General Kilpatrick, who was harassing the Rebels in their retreat, and endeavoring to cut off their trains. We could distinctly see the shells from the Federal pieces burst in the vicinity of the Monterey House. This day's march was also a trying one; worn out, and most of us with torn shoes and bleeding feet, we were urged on at our utmost speed, over slippery, stony roads, and through mud, that in many places was knee-deep. We were, besides, compelled to follow close behind a wagon train, which brought our column to a halt in every hundred yards.

Late in the evening we passed through Waynesboro, and continued marching all night without being allowed an hour of rest or sleep, and urged on in many cases, at the point of the bayonet.

At nine o'clock next morning we reached Hagerstown, but were hurried on through it to within one mile of Williamsport, Md., where we were allowed a few hours of repose. The suffering among us from fatigue and exhaustion, owing to the fearful rate at which we had been marched, and from hunger and wet, and in many cases from wounds, may readily be conceived.

All along the road from Hagerstown to Williamsport we noticed indications of General Kilpatrick's cavalry dash into Hagerstown. Our dead cavalrymen were lying in the road, and on either side of it, completely stripped of their clothing, and dead horses, broken caissons, and other remains of the conflict, were scattered here and there.

The excessive rains which had set in on the 4th, had not yet ceased,—it poured in torrents day and night. Whilst we lay near Williamsport, rations of flour and beef were distributed among us. We were, of course, compelled to do our own cooking. We roasted the beef on the end of a stick, and mixed the flour into a paste with water, and baked it on stones in front of the fire. This wretched condition of our commissariat continued unimproved during all the rest of our journey through the valley of Virginia.

On the 8th we were marched through Williamsport to the rope-ferry, on the Potomac. The river, swollen by the recent rains, was not crossable at any of the neighboring fords. This rope-ferry was, at that time, the only means the Rebels had of crossing the stream. The crossing was a slow and tedious process, though no doubt more so to the Rebels than to ourselves, for we felt that after the Potomac should be between us and our army there would be no hope of rescue, and but few opportunities for escape.

We had been told that once on Virginia soil our march to Staunton would be made by easy stages, and that the provisions furnished us would be more abundant, and of better quality. Neither of these conditions, however, was realized. All the stores which could be collected were needed by their army, and even our guards fared but little better than ourselves.

By the 11th, we had reached a place called Washington Springs, five miles from Winchester. Here we first saw, in a copy of the Richmond Enquirer, the official report of the surrender of Vicksburg to General Grant. A round of hearty cheers went up from our column, and we pushed forward on our weary journey with a lighter heart, in spite of shoeless and bleeding feet, for we knew what joy was thrilling, at that moment, the great Union heart of the nation.

On the 13th, a portion of General Imboden's command took charge of our column. The guard consisted of Captain McNeil's Partisan Rangers, Captain Patterson's Company of Cavalry, and the 61st Virginia State Militia.

We were repeatedly compelled to countermarch

through the fields, the streams which traversed the road being much swollen with the recent rains; in passing Newtown, the turnpike was impracticable, owing to this cause, and we were forced to wade waist-deep through mud and water.

By the 16th, we had reached Harrisonburg, having marched successively through Middletown, Strasburg, Woodstock, Mount Jackson, and New Market. Three miles beyond Harrisonburg we were shown a tree with an inscription upon it, which marks the spot where the Rebel, Ashby, of cavalry fame, fell the previous year.

In our march through the several towns we had often drawn upon us the wrath of the inhabitants, especially the women, who more than once taunted us with remarks not calculated to prove very gratifying to our ears. Here and there, however, a Union kerchief was waved to us from some solitary window, and sometimes a fair face would bestow upon us a commiserative glance, or a sweet voice would bid us be of good cheer.

On the morning of the 18th, our jaded column entered the town of Staunton from the Winchester road. We were a squalid set, way-worn and weary, and covered with the dust of long foot-travel; with haggard faces, and uncombed hair; some carrying their wounded arms in slings; many with bare and lacerated feet; and all bearing the unmistakable impress of the days of hunger, exposure, and fatigue, through which we had just passed. We had been marched on foot a distance of nearly two hundred miles, through the mud and the heavy rains, through the dust and under the scorching summer sun; for near three weeks we had lived chiefly on flour-paste and water; we had been swept along in hurried marches with the retreating columns of the Rebel Army through Maryland, had slept night after night under pouring rains, and had finally walked the whole length of the great Valley of Virginia, over its stony hills and through its swollen streams, to the sources of the Shenandoah. It was a beautiful country through which we had just passed, but it had presented no charms to weary eyes that were compelled to view it through a line of hostile bayonets; we felt but little sympathy for the beautiful; on our haggard countenances only this was written: "Give us rest, and food."

On the evening of the same day, our sorry column was marched through the streets of Richmond from the depot of the Virginia Central Railroad to the Libby Prison. The gloomy and forbidding exterior of the prison, and the pale, emaciated faces staring vacantly at us through the bars, were repulsive enough, but it was at least a haven of rest from the weary foot-march, and from the goad of the urging bayonet. Had we known that we were entering this loathsome prison-house not to leave it again for many, many weary days and months, more than one heart would have grown faint with a mournful presentiment, for there were among us some who were doomed never to recross its threshold as living men.

I.

1863.

July:—THE LIBBY PRISON—EARLY EXPERIENCES—A RAINY DAY—OUR COMMISSARIAT—UNPLEASANT REFLECTIONS—SCRUBBING DAY AND WHITEWASHING DAY—THE LYCEUM, AND THE LIBBY CHRONICLE—A LECTURE ON MESMERISM, AND ITS CONSEQUENCES.

THE LIBBY PRISON.

WE are now fairly launched upon the mysterious ocean of Libby life. Before embarking, however, we have had our pockets well searched by the prison warden, and everything deemed to be of a contraband nature has been confiscated. Most of us possessed but little that warranted the search, having bartered away, to obtain food, all our dispensable articles, during our sojourn in the valley of Virginia. Soon after crossing the Potomac, southward bound, there were numerous melancholy instances of a breakfast made on a pocket-knife, a dinner off a felt hat, and a supper off a pair of boots. One officer had subsisted for three days on a Colt's revolver.

The room we are in is long, low, dingy, gloomy, and suffocating. Some two hundred officers are lying packed in rows along the floor, sleeping the heavy, dreamless sleep of exhaustion. But there are some who cannot sleep; they are thinking of the camp, of home, and of friends; they are quarreling with the fortune of war; they are longing for the termination of a loathsome and hateful captivity, which has only just begun. By-and-by even the most wakeful yield to the imperative demand for rest, and with one arm for a pillow, have stretched themselves out on the bare floor.

The shadows, as they thicken on the prison walls, seem to be spreading over these long files of stirless, outstretched men, the black pall of a living death. It may be many days, many months, before the free, pure air of Heaven fans their temples again, and before the cheerful sunshine once more traces their shadows upon the green, scented grass!

The day has dawned clear and full of sunlight. I look out of the window on the James river. Immediately below is the canal; beyond it flows the river, with a rapid, murmuring current, reflecting here and there the purple flush of the morning clouds; there is a cluster of tall factories on the opposite bank; beyond these is the village of Manchester on one side, and on the other are broad fields, and the rolling hills which fringe a distant curve of the river. Looking up-stream, there is a lovely little island, three long white bridges which span the stream, half concealed by the thick foliage, and beyond these, a full mile off, is Belle Isle, with some white tents crowning an eminence. The scene is beautiful at this hour, bathed in the rich roseate mist of early morning, which pours over the gilded edges of the eastern clouds as if it overflowed from a golden vase.

I pass to another window: this one looks upon the street. Yonder building, with the barred windows, I am told, is "Castle Thunder," and on the opposite side of the street may be just seen the gable end of another prison, known by the significant title of the "Cage." Nearer is an antiquated Meeting House; then comes a negro shanty, a stable, a church, an empty lot, and a large warehouse, used as a convalescent hospital for Confederate soldiers; place behind these some rows of brick dwellings, by way of a horizon, and a pretty correct idea may be formed of what we are destined to behold every day during our sojourn here. This, with the group of tents, the headquarters of the guard, at the opposite corner of the street, and a row of sentries pacing up and down on the pavement below, is all that the windows of Libby offer in the way of an immediate prospect.

Now for the Libby itself. It stands close by the Lynchburg canal, and in full view from the river. It is a capacious warehouse, built of brick and roofed with tin. It was a busy place previous to the Rebellion; barrels and bales obstructed the stone side-walk which surrounds the building on all four of its sides; barrels and boxes were being constantly hoisted in and hoisted out; numberless boats lined the canal in front of it, and loaded drays rattled over the cobble pavement of Carey street. There was a signboard at an angle of the building, whereon you might have read in black letters on a white ground: "Libby & Sons, Ship Chandlers and Grocers." This sign-board is still at its post; but a wondrous change has come over the place. There are now no bales and boxes coming in at one end, and going out at the other; no laden boats on the canal; no drays rattling over the stone pave. There is something about it indicative of the grave, and, indeed, it *is* a sort of unnatural tomb, whose pale, wan habitants gaze vacantly out through the barred windows on the passer-by, as if they were peering from the mysterious precincts of another world.

The building has a front of about one hundred and forty feet, with a depth of about one hundred and five. There are nine rooms, each one hundred and two feet long by forty-five wide. The height of ceilings from the floor, is about seven feet; except in the upper story, which is better ventilated owing to the pitch of the roof. At each end of these rooms are five windows.

Nothing but bread has, as yet, been issued to us, half a loaf twice a day, per man. This must be washed down with James River water, drawn from a hydrant over the wash-trough. To-morrow, we are to be indulged with the luxury of bacon-soup.

There are some filthy blankets hanging about the room; they have been used time and again by the many who have preceded us; they are soiled, worn, and filled with vermin, but we are recommended to help ourselves in time; if we do so with reluctance and profound disgust it is because we are now more particular than we will be by-and-by.

We have tasted of the promised soup: it is boiled water sprinkled with rice, and seasoned with the rank juices of stale bacon; we must shut our eyes to eat it; the bacon, I have no doubt, might have walked into the pot of its own accord. It is brought up to us in wooden buckets, and we eat it, in most cases without spoons, out of tin-cups. "Quis custodiet ipsos custodes?"

It has been raining for several days. How much more gloomy the prison looks, robbed of the little scattering sunlight which, on clear days, comes creeping timidly in between the window-bars! The effect on the minds of all in the prison is very perceptible: there is a tendency to lie about on the floor, to grumble, to be irritable, to have the blues. No wonder. The little ration of sunshine which Heaven is wont to issue to us is cut off. There is, here, something delightful in letting a ray of sparkling sunshine fall upon one's face; you can sit and look at it for hours. The pleasure which it affords is not difficult to account for: this sunlight comes from the sky, pure, and untainted; it comes, free and unshackled, from without; it is a link between the captive and that liberty which he has learned to prize so dearly; it is a golden bridge over which his thoughts, rendered morbid by gloomy reveries, pass out through the prison-bars, and go forth into the free realm of space, to wander wheresoever they will.

The rain pattering on the tin roof overhead has a mournful sound. It is singular how this music of the beating rain will always carry one back, far back, into child-life; it is apt to have a strange, sad influence on us whenever we hear it; but nowhere so strange, nor so sad, as in a prison.

We have received permission to purchase provisions

Libby Prison.

outside the prison. We have elected an officer, of the Quartermasters' Department, to be our "Commissary-in-Chief." He has divided us into messes of fifteen to twenty, and we are to do our own cooking; stoves are being put up, and the cook-room partitioned off. It is a great privilege to be allowed to cook for ourselves! An assistant commissary is elected for each mess: to these the chief commissary issues, and they in their turn issue to the cooks. The hours are so distributed that more than two hundred may be able to cook on two small stoves. The prison authorities issue meat and rice, of which we will make soup; with the boiled meat from the soup a hash will be made for breakfast next morning. All extras will be at the expense of individuals. Rye Coffee sells at one dollar per pound; sugar, three dollars; eggs, two dollars per dozen; butter, four dollars per pound.—So much for our culinary prospects.

The officers of the gunboats "Satellite" and "Reliance" are now with us. It is humorously rumored in the prison that they were captured by a desperate charge of the Rebel *cavalry* on the gunboats. These jolly tars will suffer less than the landsmen from their imprisonment; they have only to imagine themselves in the hold of some huge three-decker, during a dead calm.

There has been much excitement in the city about a rumored movement of Federal troops up the Peninsula with the design of capturing the capital; the bells all over the city were rung this morning, and only a few moments ago, being attracted to the window by an unusual rattling of wheels on the street, we had a glimpse of one of the celebrated "Mule Batteries" which fulmine over Rebeldom, and whose bellicose braying is no doubt destined to strike terror into the hearts of the northern *barbarians*.

It is difficult for one who has never before been compelled to look out upon the world from behind the bars of a prison, to convince himself of the fact that he is really deprived of his liberty. There is a merry group of children, romping and playing near the river; I listen to their joyous laughter, and, somehow, it has a very mournful sound. Most people have sighed, at times, to be young again; that sigh is a longer and a deeper one when we yearn, not only for the happy *insouciance* of childhood, but for its freedom also. These thoughtless little ones romping and laughing under the very windows of our prison-house; these happy hearts beating quick with the excitement of their merry sport in the pleasant shadows of a summer afternoon, how near are they to other and older hearts which are heavy with the gloom of captivity. But is not this after all a counter-part of the great world, in which, Mde. De Staël remarks, one half is always laughing at the other half? Truly: **joy and sorrow, good** and evil, how near grow they to one another in the vale of human life! The passers-by on the pave below, with what indifference they glance up at the pale faces that peer out between the bars!

These are not the pleasantest reflections in the world, but they are such as force themselves upon the mind of a prisoner. When Hood wrote in the "Bridge of Sighs" the line "Anywhere, anywhere, out of the world," he must have been thinking of a place not much worse than this we are now in. I can imagine a "Convict Ship" on its way to Australia—far out in mid-ocean—with nothing but a limitless waste of blue water around it, and nothing but a limitless waste of blue air above it—and crowded with sorrowing human beings. It seems to me that this prison bears some resemblance to it. We are indeed much like so many passengers, who feel that in a common danger and a common fate, there is much that creates a mutual interest. Our ship-simile might be carried very far, but it is too vivid to be pleasant. Ours is a voyage, not of pleasure, but of necessity; there is no convivial wine in our locker over which to toast the friends we love, and wherein to drown the tedium of the journey; we are on short, very short rations; and, to replace sea-sickness, we have a fearful substitute in home-sickness, by far the more trying of the two.

I am interrupted in my profound reflections by the sudden influx into the room of a dozen negroes carrying buckets and brooms. I know but too well what this portends. It is scrubbing-day. These are the clouds which portend the storm.

All that has ever been written, grumbled, or soliloquized, by forlorn and outraged husbands driven from the sanctity of their homes on those dismal occasions when their demented spouses have been seized with the "scrubbing-fever," and have pulled up all the carpets in the house, and crowded the furniture in pyramidal confusion in all the by-ways, and have lathered the floors, and the stairs, and the windows, and have rendered the entire premises fit to be inhabited, for the next twenty-four hours, only by improbable web-footed husbands of aquatic propensities,—when the flying spray of soap and water is dashed into their faces even from the doors of their private *sanctums*, and splashed over their best beaver from the parlor window-panes,—when, in fine, the whole female household seems to have gone stark mad with an irrepressible insanity for soap-suds,— all, I repeat, that has ever been uttered, under circumstances so aggravating, by exasperated husbands, cannot do justice to a scrubbing-day in the Libby. For the anti-lavatory husband can at least, when hotly pressed by the enemy, make good his retreat out of the front door: here, there is no line of escape! Everything, pretty much, that you possess, your bed, your baggage, and your dinner, are on the floor, and that floor, will be in a few moments a tempestuous ocean of splashing, filthy water. You may baffle the foe, perhaps, for a short time, by rapid and well-conducted retreats to little islands of dry floor here and there, where you stand on tip-toe, your blanket over your shoulders, your day's rations in one hand, and your coffee-pot in the other; but you will, finally, be compelled to surrender, and resign yourself to your watery fate.

There is only one other day, with us, which can, in any manner compare with the tortures and the terrors of this: that is, "whitewashing" day. You are then harassed, not from below, but from above; this operation seems to have been invented by the fiendish ingenuity of some monster in human shape, for the express purpose of completing the ruin of your already dilapidated wardrobe. Your only coat is sure to come out of the ordeal spotted and streaked with white down the back; your only hat will look as if you had just come in from a severe snow-storm, and you will walk about the rest of the day like a sort of hitherto undiscovered specimen of the Leopard family, deeming yourself fortunate enough, if you do not create a, to you, unaccountable laugh wherever you go, by a snow-flake of lime glued on to the end of your nose.

In order to while away, to some extent, the tedium of our monotonous life, we have, among other pastimes, organized a Lyceum, or Debating Club. The scenes which it, at times presents, are worthy the graphic pencil of an artist. The chairman sits on the floor *á la Turque*, the "chair" itself being an empty name, without any local existence. The members sit in a circle on the floor, like Indian Chiefs at a war council.

The debates are very spirited, and grave questions, involving the destinies of the whole human race, and the future destiny of "Our great Country," are discussed with intense enthusiasm, sometimes even with political virulence, and not seldom with very bad grammar.

An eloquent orator, naked to the waist [for the weather is very warm], rises on his bare feet, and flourishes his sleeveless arms about in a style as imposing and forcible as it is original. He is portraying, with the glowing and picturesque colors of an inspired imagination, the sublime beauties of the ancient philosophy. He is patriotically suicidal with Socrates; suicidally heroic with Cato; astutely critical with Horace; mysteriously profound with Seneca, and profoundly mysterious with Cicero, when he is ludicrously interrupted by a vociferous call from the cook-house, of "Fall in, small messes, for your black beans!" A shrewd debater on the negative side of the question, taking immediate advantage of this laughable interruption, rises promptly and obtains the "floor." He reviews rapidly, but with remarkable perspicacity, the fallacious arguments of his shirtless predecessor; overturns the illogical conclusions to which "the gentleman on the affirmative side who has just addressed you," would lead the intelligent members of the Association; scatters to the four winds of Heaven all the philosophy of the past, all the philosophy of the present, and all the philosophy of the future; and, in conclusion, triumphantly calls the attention of the learned chairman to the scanty wardrobe of his misguided opponent, as circumstantially corroborative of the scantiness of his wit.

All this is quite comical and perfectly harmless, and aids admirably in passing away the time; no one would think, therefore, of discountenancing the "Lyceum." Besides, it publishes a newspaper, called the "Libby Chronicle," which is edited by a witty and intelligent chaplain, and which descants with considerable acumen upon the various occurrences of our prison-life. When the reading of the Chronicle is announced throughout the building, which occurs, generally, once a week, there is a great rush to listen to its contents. The audience collects in a circle on the floor, and the Editor, standing in the centre, reads the various articles from the slips of paper on which they have been written. This mode of publication, besides being quite economical, is decidedly sociable.

One of the officers lectures to us, on the subject of mesmerism. He tells us about the electric fluid which permeates all space, about clairvoyance, about the magnetic spheres, and about many other interesting facts connected with the mesmeric science. The fact, whether mesmerism be a *science*, however, is caviled at by some of the medical faculty present, and at the succeeding meeting of the Lyceum, the all-important question: "Is Mesmerism a *true* science?" is discussed with much warmth, and at great length. The Faculty being reinforced by an astute correspondent of the New York Tribune, assail the mesmeric party with redoubled energy, and finally, so much is said, on both sides, that the learned chairman of the Debating Association, bewildered at first by the rapid discharges, from the opposing batteries, of all sorts of technical canister and scientific grape, and lost, soon afterwards, in a labyrinth of anatomical dissertations and a complication of magnetic incomprehensibilities, is drawn into a vortex of irretrievable confusion, and, ere the close of the meeting, is seized with the frightful hallucination that he is attempting the desperate feat of walking over Niagara Falls on a telegraph wire, with a twelve jar galvanic battery in full blast in his coat-tail pocket!

The mesmeric excitement gains ground with alarming rapidity, and soon becomes general; all sorts of impromptu mesmerisers may be seen here and there about the rooms, surrounded by anxious and serious groups, and endeavoring, with all the earnestness of mesmeric faith, to worry suspected mediums into an impossible sleep. It is shrewdly argued by some that a state of chronic somnolency would be an admirable mental condition in which to pass through the horrors of a protracted captivity; and that, as by mesmeric influence, all kinds of hallucinations may be produced on the brain of the sleeper, nothing would be easier than to eat stale bread and imagine it to be sponge-cake; to turn James River water into sparkling champagne; and to convert into "Floating islands" the vapid juices of weak bean soup! These admirable results, and the startling phenomena which accompany them, however, are, unfortunately for us, not obtained; the medium, in spite of him, cannot hear anything of the luxurious jingle of silver about his smutted tin-cup, and the same old prison-odor of superannuated bacon still clings, with anti-mesmeric tenacity, to the incorrigible vapors of the cook-house.

CONFEDERATE GUERRILLAS.

The Tub.

II.

1863.

August:—KILLING TIME—THE NEW ARRIVAL—EXPERIENCES OF A "FRESH FISH"—EPISODES OF DAILY LIFE—A PRAYER—STARVATION—ABOUT A TUB—A MOCK TRIAL.

KILLING TIME.

I AM repeatedly struck by the fact of how much prisoners become like children. The importance of momentous events is given to the merest trifles, and in order to elicit that most contrary and problematical result ironically styled *killing* time, recourse is had to the most insignificant and primitive pastimes. Unwearable finger rings, and sacrilegious looking crosses are sawed and filed out of ration bones; the handles of brushes and the backs of combs are carved with touching mottoes; gray heads become speculative over jack-straws; and, sedate and dignified patriots indulge in the grotesque antics of "leap-frog." Then, to see them crowding up, tin-cup in hand, to receive the meagre allowance of pale, ambiguous soup; to watch them lying about the floor in unique groups, or sauntering through the rooms, bored to death with ennui,—a host of shoeless, shirtless, shameless spectres, each one wandering wildly about in the preposterous effort to get away from himself!

It is laughable—and in that mirth there is a moral—to see a brigadier-general, sitting down philosophically to peel onions for a stew; a colonel of cavalry, sweeping the floor; or, a Division Quartermaster in carpet slippers, and become irascible in a violent controversy about the distribution of spoons!

There is a new arrival of prisoners. The cry is started of "more Yanks!" "Fresh Fish!" and there is a general rush to the windows to obtain a glimpse of the new-comers, followed, in all likelihood, by a spirited interchange of amicable recognitions.

The "Fresh Fish" are taken into the lower passage, where they are formed in line, their names registered, and their pockets searched. They are then, if they be officers, conducted up-stairs into their future domicil, and, if enlisted men, into a lower room, or they are sent to Belle Isle, or to one of the other prisons in Richmond.

In the general thirst for the latest news, the hapless "Fresh Fish" who just enters, is beset by the whole bevy of jail-birds, whose haggard countenances, dishevelled hair, and supernatural attire, are sufficient to inspire him with feelings not the most enviable, either as to his personal safety for the present, or as to his personal comfort for the future. A number of questions are asked him, all at the same time, whilst one pulls him this way, and another that:— "What news from the Army of the Potomac?" "Where is such a Corps, or such a Division?" "When were you captured?" "*Where* were you captured?" *How* were you captured?" And so on for a quarter of an hour, until at last the poor fellow, breathless and exhausted, drops his haversack out of one hand, and his coat out of the other, that he may wipe away the torrents of perspiration that stream down his face. There is then a commiserative counter-cry of "give him air!" "don't crowd him!" and so forth, during another period of noise and confusion. At length the unfortunate man recovers his breath, and silence is enforced, that not a word falling from his lips may be lost, when he informs the gaping listeners, to their utter discomfiture and dismay, that he comes from the southwest, and was captured five months ago! This provoking revelation is likely to elicit some such charitable suggestion as "put that fellow out!" which being impracticable under the circumstances is probably modified to "dip him in the bath-tub!"

Once let alone, the new arrival proceeds to

enquire about his "quarters," a term which he soon discovers is only applied by courtesy to six feet by two of bare floor; he is perhaps furnished, in addition, with a blanket which many a captive has here, during the past two years, wrapped like a "martial cloak around him," and which is pretty sure to be colonized. Being now provided for, to the full extent of the prison charity, and having sauntered about the rooms to satisfy his curiosity as to the peculiar features of his new abode, he finally stretches himself out on his "six by two," arranges his haversack comfortably under his head, and does precisely what all the new arrivals have done before him: he begins to *think*.

Just at the culminating point of some wild revery about his far-off wife and innocent babes, he is suddenly aroused by a terrific commotion in the room; the prisoners, with a savage halloo, are rushing frantically to the windows. What can it mean? "What *is* the matter?" asks the new arrival, as he springs to his feet, in accents tremulous with the excitement of terror. Will no one tell him? no; every one is in a hurry, and no one tells him. The most frightful suspicions dart through his brain. Have the prisoners mutinied, and are they slaughtering the guards? He has read a barbarous article in the "*Richmond Enquirer*" about retaliation, and the raising of the black flag—no! would they dare to—and he grasps his throat convulsively. Perhaps the building is on fire. A horrible thought! Five hundred human beings struggling through one contracted doorway! The alarming narrowness of the staircase also recurs vividly to his memory. He rushes madly after the crowd; in his blind career he treads upon the countenance of a slumbering convalescent, and materially retards the recovery of the afflicted man; or he puts his foot into a coffee-pot and overturns its contents; or ruins some choice and expensive preparation of stewed apples; or plays the deuce with some valuable collection of tin-ware, thereby subjecting himself to the violent abuse of a "private mess." At length, after much spirited elbowing, during which he regrets the necessity of being rough upon a reverend member of the clergy, he finally reaches a window. Are the prisoners leaping madly into the street to avert an agonizing death amid the flames? This would be a fearful alternative for a man with a far-off wife and innocent babes! By a desperate effort he obtains a full view of the street; the extraordinary commotion is satisfactorily accounted for. He laughs outright. The frightful phantoms which haunted his brain but a moment since, have fled. He beholds the mysterious cause of this wild excitement: it is a woman passing along the pavement below.

So he goes sauntering back to his "six-by-two," a wiser, if not a better man.

As night approaches, the situation of the fresh arrival becomes somewhat critical. He succeeds, after awhile, in bringing about a not altogether satisfactory compromise between his blanket, his haversack, and himself; after lying, first on one side, then on the other, then on his back, and then on no side in particular, he finally falls into an ambiguous slumber, and dreams unutterable miseries. But he has not yet emptied to the dregs the bitter cup of his first day's experience in the Libby. In the midst of a thrilling night-mare, he is awakened by startling and confused yells in the distance; they approach, rendering the night hideous with their echoes; nearer and nearer they come, repeated at short intervals, by weird voices, and wafted up from the street by the night wind. But this suspense becomes insupportable; he leaps to his feet, and makes his way to the nearest window; it is raining, and the sidewalk below is shrouded in impenetrable darkness, but a shrill Confederate voice informs him, as it takes up in piercing accents the diabolical refrain, that it is "Twelve o'clock," and that at "Post No. 10, all's well!" This gratifying intelligence restores the alarmed prisoner's presence of mind, and chastened and subdued by the Christian-like resignation and buoyancy of spirits of "Post No. 10," he once more returns to torture himself into an unresolvable problem of chaotic anatomy, and falls asleep for the last time that night, with the pleasing reflection that to-morrow, thank Heaven, he will have ceased to be a "Fresh Fish!"

The first thing we hear in the morning is the stentorian voice of a certain fertile colored genius, familiarly known in Libby as "Old Ben." This voice daily announces to the half-awakened prisoners that there is "great news in de papers! Talagraphic dispatches from ebery whar! *Kase* I'm bound to trabel!"

Old Ben is followed by "the General," another colored attaché of the prison, whose chief duty is to go through the rooms every morning and fumigate them with tar-smoke. The "General" is a staunch supporter of the old flag, and qualifies his fumigatory process by calling it "a good Union smoke!"

The next announcement is, that of "Mess number so-and-so—breakfast!" There is then a general rush of the members of said mess to their morning repast, which is spread in true alms-house style, upon a long, bare, pine table. To the casual observer, the meal would appear to consist wholly of deformed tin plates and pewter spoons, but an oniony odor which pervades the premises is a welcome earnest of "hash" to come. If a newly arrived member in the mess has been unfortunate enough to oversleep himself—which will never occur to him *twice*—he may rest assured that his slumbers will not be disturbed; this would be the very height of madness, because, by a shrew algebraic calculation, we arrive at the following gratifying result:

$a =$ total members of mess.
$b =$ slumbering ditto of ditto.
$x =$ rations of hash.

Now then, we have the quantities $1^b - 1^x$, and $20^a - 1^b$, from which will naturally be deduced the following equation:

$$20^a - 1^b = 19^a + 19^x + 1^x.$$

Various little episodes diversify the monotony of Libby life. There are two roll-calls daily, when the prisoners are counted; there is the Sergeant, who every morning conjures up a host of dilapidated spectres with the necromantic words, "Fall in, sick, and go down"—which means down to the Surgeon's office—but which the uninitiated might imagine to imply a diabolical desire, on the part of the Confederate authorities, that the sick might fall into some dreadful place—perhaps the canal—and *go down* never to rise again.

Each prisoner must serve his tour at policing, and putting things in order, during which he is in all likelihood dispatched by the chief commissary on a spirited reconnoissance in quest of secreted spoons. Of course there is your little washing to be done, also; you rub and soap away for dear life, like a male washer-woman, and the difficulty of getting things to look clean teaches you a wholesome lesson; you learn thereby to duly appreciate the merit of lavatory labors, and you behold in all its glaring monstrosity that mean and criminal practice of palming off counterfeit six-pences upon hard-working laundresses.

The last days of summer!—All our hopes of being exchanged or paroled, have been dissipated one after another, and our captivity is passing with rapid strides from the last green of summer to the sere yellow of autumn; from faint hope to settled despair. Rumors of battles which are being fought, and of victories which are being won, reach us from time to time, and cheer us in our seclusion. The hopes of the Confederacy are paling fast, and its social status, if we may judge by that of the capital as portrayed in its daily journals, deteriorates with a steady downward course that must soon lead to utter anarchy.

Among the prisoners are quite a number of chaplains. This time the rude grasp of Mars has not respected the inviolable sanctity of the holy robe. Sermons, and prayer-meetings are of frequent occurrence; the minister takes his position in the centre of the room, and the congregation sit, or kneel, around him on the floor. It is a service well befitting the prison-house, with its prospects of long suffering and self-denial, and its menaces of weary hours, and days of languishing tedium. The spirit of the Almighty is ardently invoked to descend to us in our gloomy abode; to pour the sunshine of Its glory upon the dismal prison-walls, and the balm of Its mercy into the weary heart; to give to the mind of Its holy strength, that looking wistfully out through the prison-bars at the light and the liberty without, the captive may temper his complainings with faith, and his despair with hope.

In the room under the one we occupy, are confined a large number of Federal non-commissioned officers, and citizens captured in Maryland and Pennsylvania during the late invasion by General Lee's Army. They are even more poorly fed than ourselves. Through a chink in the floor we pass them down crackers, and pieces of bread, whenever we can spare them from our own slender store. It is pitiful to see these starving men struggling with their thin, lank hands, at the hole, to catch the bits we drop through to them. We often see them fight desperately over a morsel of bread, even beating and knocking one another down. I never look through that chink, but I can see below some anxious, wasted face, and a pair of sunken eyes, peering up in wistful supplication for a crust! The Confederate authorities assert that they are doing all they can for us! If unavoidable, this system of starvation would be frightful enough: if intentional, it is too revoltingly cruel to ever meet with its full punishment upon earth.

The water we use, is drawn at a hydrant, under which a bath-tub, or rather *trough*, has been constructed, which serves for all washing purposes generally. This tub, which would under ordinary conditions of comfort inconveniently hold one bather, is often made to accommodate three or four at a time, with a crowd in waiting and ready to squeeze in at the first opportunity. A misty spray of muddy soap and water constantly envelopes the tub, so that it presents somewhat the appearance of a rock by the sea-side, against which the rising waves dash themselves incessantly. In this unusually hot weather the prison is heated into a huge oven, in which several hundred human beings are thoroughly baked in the most approved style of a first class steam bakery. Of course under such circumstances, the pressure upon the tub is tremendous—for it is a well in the prison-sands, and the splashing and spluttering which take place there, may readily be conceived.

A prisoner lately arrived, and not yet well acquainted with the prison rules, was, some days ago, anxious to take a bath, and wash away the accumulated dust and mud gathered during a journey from the banks of the Rappahannock. After several abortive efforts to achieve an ablution, he shrewdly resolved to wait until after dark, and in the silence and secrecy of the midnight hour, when all should be soundly asleep, to creep stealthily to the tub, take triumphant possession, and scour himself to his heart's content.

Night creeps on apace; one by one the bathers retire; the "all's well!" is cried by the sentries; the prisoners are all asleep, laid out snugly side by side over the whole superficial extent of the floor, as if it were an unearthed cemetery originally distributed into private lots; a variety of naso-orchestral sounds, alone breaks the profound stillness of the hour. Everything proving propitious, the "newly arrived," rises, on tiptoe, soap and towel in hand; steps out cautiously between the heads of the sleepers; takes breath and steps again, within the eighth of an inch of a captain's ear; next plants his bare heel within a hair's breadth of a colonel's nose; steps forward carefully again and feels something soft under his foot,—easy! it is the head of a second lieutenant of cavalry. He has at length reached, in comparative safety, a window which is near the tub,—is startled by the intoxicated appearance of the moon, just seen looming above the horizon, and no doubt staggering down to bed with a glass too many in her head; he experiences a half superstitious and guilty feeling. Finally the tub is reached, and the goal won. With a tremulous hand he turns the water on:

fizz! froth! splash! out it comes, gushing in a powerful stream. What a thundering noise it makes in the stillness of the night! a cry goes up from among the awakened sleepers; a fearful cry, followed by loud yells, and shouts of "Stop that water!" "Come out of that tub!" "Strike a light!" "Boot him! boot him!" If any doubt is created in the mind of the terrified bather as to the precise definition of the last exclamation, this doubt is soon dispelled by the storm of heterogeneous missiles, which pour upon him from every quarter of the room; panic-stricken and unable to understand the meaning of the frightful uproar he has originated, and only able to comprehend distinctly that he is the radical cause of it, by the boot which whistles past his nose in fearful proximity like a grape shot, and by the broomstick, which cuts him across the legs in the manner of "rail road iron." He makes his way back as best he can to his blanket, never stopping, of course, to check the water. The tumult in consequence, increases, and there is, finally, a general rush to the tub to seize the offender. The greatest confusion prevails in the room. "Who is it?" "Stop that water!" "Put him out!" "Strike a light!" A light is struck, and a large crowd has gathered about the tub.

It is, of course, found empty. Loud denunciations are uttered, accompanied with violent threats of bringing the offender to justice, whilst the half distracted cause of all this mischief, lies closely enveloped in his blanket, snoring with unnatural ferocity.

Gradually the tumult ceases, and ere long, all are gathered once more to slumber under the raven's wing. There is one, however, who sleeps not,—it is the "new arrival." "Why should I have created such a diabolical commotion?" he asks of himself. "I am sure I was only going to take a bath, without doing a particle of harm to any one." Yes, poor fellow! you are "green" yet in the prison. You do not know that it is one of the strictest rules here that the wash tub shall not be used after 9 P. M.; you little think you have been guilty of a crime, the penalty for which is to be locked up in the dungeon for a week on bread and water!

There is a certain captain who is a great stickler for the enforcement of prison rules and regulations—a dignified and retiring gentleman, and a great favorite. He is very severe on the subject of the tub, near which he sleeps. Woe unto the offender who turns on the water after nine P. M. All are in the habit of looking up to the captain on the subject of the tub; it is his favorite battle ground, and all are too cognizant of the astuteness of his strategy to risk a nocturnal skirmish with him. Many will long remember one memorable night in which he attacked no less a personage than a full quartermaster, and after a bloody and obstinate conflict, routed him with great slaughter, cutting off his communications, and capturing his trains. This action is humorously related in the prison as "The Battle of the Tub."

Not the least amusing incident to which the tempestuous history of this devoted tub has given rise, is the trial by a mock court of one of the most discreet and dignified of the officers, charged with endangering the peace and discipline of the prison community, by an attempt somewhat of the nature of the one just related, to enjoy the secret raptures of a clandestine bath. Much humor and mirth were created by this comical trial. A gray headed cavalry officer acted as judge upon the occasion, and the mock gravity and professional air he assumed, as well as his shrewd wit, convulsed the court with laughter during the proceedings.

The empanelling of the jury was rendered amusingly

difficult by the fact that nearly all who were subpœnaed had been selected out of the foreign element: French, Germans, and Hungarians, especially those who knew but little of the language. The accused of course became the target at which all the mischievous witticisms were aimed; but he bore himself throughout the trying ordeal with the most admirable good-nature. Among the many amusing arguments urged by the defence was one, sustained by powerful evidence, that the accused had never been known even, to wash his face, since his arrival in the prison; one of the Faculty was produced who testified to the effect that the accused suffered from frequent attacks of hydrophobia; another in assisting him to an alibi, testified that he had seen the prisoner on the night in question coming out of an ice-cream saloon on Main street, in Richmond, with a Confederate lady on his arm; a fragment of a letter had been picked up by another, near the tub, signed by one "Susan," the contents of which aspersed the fidelity of the aged warrior, and brought to light some highly amusing incidents of his amatory experiences. The prisoner at the bar listened to these jokes with charming good temper, and none seemed to relish more than himself the drollery of the whole affair.

A verdict of "guilty" was brought in, with a recommendation to the mercy of the court; and the sentence, which terminated the proceedings, was to the effect that the accused should be drummed out of the prison into the Federal lines, and that, in view of the recommendation to mercy, the prosecution should pay all the costs!

OLD "SMOKE."

A future Brigadier.

III.

1863.

September:—Amatory—The Catechism—Nocturnal Sports—The fate of a Union Officer charged with being a Spy—Distribution of Rooms.

AMATORY.

———•———

THAT felicitous German author, Weber, in his "Lachenden Philosophen," relates of an Italian lady that she was heard to express the wish that ice cream might be *forbidden*—it would taste so much better! It was no contemptible philosophy, this of the fair Italian; for, what an exaggerated value do we not at times attach, even to the merest trifles, simply because they are inaccessible to us. This spirit of contradiction is wonderfully developed by the quasi-barbaric existence we lead here, what though the yearnings of our palates are far less luxurious than those of the Italian Donna,—ice cream and other delicate confections taking up no room where so many of the simplest accessories of civilized life are lacking. Indeed it is not so much the famine of food for the body, as that for the mind, which lays so stubborn a siege to the philosophic patience of the many. We may be resigned to be fed, physically, upon anything; but when the mind is in question one is apt to be less easily satisfied. **Ah, yes!** The heart yearns for its home-confections, its social sherbets, its amorous Heidsick!

I have been led into these profound reflections by the serio-comic, semi-tragic manner in which I have seen several photographs tremulously extracted from newly received letters, and by the mercurial manner in which the restless recipient, with an absolutely transparent effort at *nonchalance*, and an ill-feigned simplicity of purpose, wanders about the room with one hand suspiciously inserted in his breast pocket, seeking for some recondite corner where with the pretty treasure concealed in a book, he may decoy all passers-by into the impression that he is absorbed in the paradigms of his French Grammar, or in the touching mysteries of "Aurora Floyd." As he sits there, dreaming over the faithful counterpart of a pair of sentimental blue eyes, the graceful sweep of an arching eyebrow, or the amorous pout of a suggestive mouth,—such a youth is, I dare say, highly to be envied; for, one of those weird little birds, with beaks of gold and wings of purple, which haunt the heart-world and warble such pleasant music in the ears of parted lovers, is no doubt singing sweet tunes to him, perched in a reckless curl of his unpomatumed hair!

Let me not be deemed guilty of a breach of prison confidence, or of limning in colors too trivial the stormy sorrows of the heart; rather than brood over such woes—a practice which only tends to render the mind of the prisoner morbid and misanthropic—far better is it to gild the storm-cloud with the faint sunshine of a patient smile.

One of the most original institutions among the prisoners is that practiced every night, after the lights are put out. It is styled "the catechism." It consists of a series of satirical, critical, serio-comic interrogatories, referring either to events of recent occurrence in the prison, or to incidents connected with the previous experiences of some of the officers; they are invariably personal in their application, and wo unto him who falls into the clutches of these nocturnal catechisers, or who attempts to remonstrate against so popular an amusement. Such significant questions are asked as "Who hid behind the big gun?" "Who has Brigadier on the brain?" "Who washed his clothes in the soup bucket?" "Who surrendered for humanity's sake?" and these are replied to with the names of the several offenders much to the *gusto* of those acquainted with the circumstances referred to.

This more original than intellectual amusement is occasionally varied by a sequence of hideous imitations of all known fowls and quadrupeds, with a menagerie-like effect which would not sound unnatural in a virgin forest of central Africa.

These highly refined entertainments invariably terminate with a grand bombardment, by way of a *finale à la militaire*, during which all kinds of missiles, even to the fragments of stale corn-bread, are violently and rapidly discharged from numberless masked batteries and go whirring all over the room, crashing among the tin-ware, and barrels, and boxes, with a continuous rattle which quite reminds one of a brisk skirmish, and is not unaccompanied with some serious apprehensions as to the safety of uncovered heads.

A gloom has hung over our prison community for some days past, owing to the appearance in the Richmond papers, of the letter and local item transcribed below:

"CASTLE THUNDER, RICHMOND, VIRGINIA,
September 23d, 1863.
"DEAR FATHER:—By permission and through the courtesy of Captain Alexander, I am enabled to write

you a few lines. You, who before this have heard from me in regard to my situation here, can, I trust bear it, when I tell you that my days on earth are soon ended.

"Last Saturday I was court-martialled, and this evening, a short time since, I received notice of my sentence by Captain Alexander, who has since shown me every kindness consistent with his duty.

"Writing to my dear parents, I feel there can be no greater comfort after such tidings than to tell you that I trust, by the mercy of our Heavenly Father, to die the death of a Christian.

"For more than a year, since the commencement of my confinement, I have been trying to serve Him in my own feeble way, and I do not fear to go to Him.

"I would have loved to see you all again; God saw best not; why should we mourn? Comfort your hearts, my dear parents, by thoughts of God's mercy unto your son, and bow with reverence beneath the hand of Him who 'doeth all things well.'

"* * I sent a ring to my wife by a clergyman, Monday last; I also sent a telegram to yourself, which will arrive too late, as the time of my execution is set for the day after to-morrow.

"Dear parents: There are but a few more moments left me; I will try to think often of you, God bless and comfort you; remember me kindly and respectfully to all my dear friends and relatives. Tell Kitty I hope to meet her again. Take care of Freddy for me; put him often in remembrance of me.

"Dear mother, good-bye. God comfort you, my mother, and bless you with the love of happy children. Farewell, my father; we meet again by God's mercy.

"SPENCER KELLOGG."

"At eleven o'clock yesterday forenoon a detail of one hundred men from the City Battalion, marched from Castle Thunder with Spencer Kellogg, the recently condemned spy, in custody.

"The cavalcade reached the scene of execution about half-past twelve o'clock, where, as usual, a vast concourse of people, of both sexes and all ages, were congregated. After a few moments spent in preliminary arrangements, the prisoner was escorted, under guard, to the gallows. While seated in the hack awaiting the perfection of the arrangements for his execution, he conversed gaily, with the utmost *nonchalance* with Dr. Burrows, frequently smiling at some remark made either by himself or the minister.

"Arriving under the gallows, the charges preferred against the accused and the sentence of the court-martial were read. A short but impressive prayer was then offered by the minister, at the conclusion of which the condemned man, unaccompanied, mounted the scaffold.

"In a few moments Detective Capehart followed, and commenced to adjust the rope over the neck of the condemned, in which he assisted, all the while talking with the officer. On taking off his hat, to admit the noose over his head, he threw it one side, and, falling off the scaffold, it struck a gentleman beneath, when the prisoner turned quickly, and bowing, said: 'excuse me, sir!'

"A negro next came on the scaffold with a ladder, and proceeded to fasten the rope to the upper beam, the prisoner meanwhile regarding him with the greatest composure. The rope being fastened, the negro was in the act of coming down, when the prisoner, looking up at the rope, remarked: 'This will not break my neck! It is not more than a foot fall! Doctor, I wish you would come up and arrange this thing!' The rope was then arranged to his satisfaction, and the cloth cap placed over his head.

"The condemned man then bowed his head, and engaged a few seconds in prayer, at the conclusion of which he raised himself, and standing perfectly erect, pronounced in a clear voice: 'All ready!'

"The drop fell, and the condemned man was launched into Eternity!"

Kellogg was a man of prepossessing appearance. His skin, from his long confinement, some fifteen months, had become as fair and delicate as a girl's. He was about thirty-five years of age. He was accused of having gone into the Confederate Engineer Corps, at Island Number Ten, for the purpose of gaining information for the benefit of the Federal Government, and is said by his captors to have died with the conviction that he had furnished more valuable information, in the character of a spy, to that Government, than any other ten men in the United States service. These facts have been denied by the friends of Kellogg at the North, who assert that he was innocent of the charge. Surely, he died with that calm heroic courage which wins the admiration of every true soldier. Poor Kellogg! It will be a worthier hand than mine which shall write your name on that page of your country's history, which records the story of the martyr, and the fallen brave!

We have been largely reinforced, by General Bragg, with a host of prisoners from Chickamauga. Seven rooms in the building, besides one other, used as a hospital, are now filled with Federal officers, numbering in all, near one thousand. The officers belonging to the armies of the Potomac and Cumberland, and those of General Milroy's and Colonel Streight's command, occupy separate rooms. We have now the upper and lower, (second and third stories,) east rooms, the first floor and basement being assigned to the hospital; these are occupied by the officers of the Potomac army;—the upper and lower middle rooms, are occupied by the officers of the Cumberland army, the lower floor being used as a general kitchen;—and in the upper and lower west rooms, are confined the officers of Milroy's and Streight's command. The middle rooms are familiarly known as "Chickamauga."

When asked where we "live," we answer, for instance, "north west corner, upper east room," or "such post, or window, lower west room." Our community has assumed imposing proportions; it is a rapidly growing colony and represents nearly every state in the Union.

IMPROVISED LAMP.

"Five for a Dollar"

IV.

1863.

October:—Preparing for Winter—Sports—The Election—A Yankee Trick.

PREPARING FOR WINTER.

AS the cool weather gains upon us, lying about on the bare floor, *en deshabille*, must be foregone. It has never entered into the calculations of our keepers to furnish our prison-home for us; so, we must set to work, and by a desperate effort of our ingenuity, furnish it ourselves. Every day I observe great improvements in this department of our housekeeping; diminutive, unpretending stools, made from spare ends of shelf-boards and blanket racks, have given way to more aspiring attempts at chairs; boxes from home have been worried into rickety, phthisical looking little tables, or hung up to serve as cupboards; commissary barrels have been sawed and hammered into unsightly, and somewhat uneasy "easy-chairs;" a stray piece of blanket makes, here and there, a tolerable table-cloth; a suspended barrel hoop replaces the long lost luxury of a clothes perch; a splinter forced into the wall in the interstices between the bricks, will support your hat in a cheap and decorous manner; an empty can, once the receptacle of some highly prized delicacy, makes an admirable lamp, in which, with a wick made from the nether extremity of a cotton garment, and fed with the waste fat of sundry pork rations, diffuses a fair amount of light, backed by its compound metallic reflector. With a seat, a table, and a lamp, at the prisoner's disposal, the long winter evenings will not find him totally unprepared. Indeed there is at times experienced in the midst of the long room, scattered all over with little squatter-like colonies gathered round a cluster of their rude furniture and pork-fat lamps, a something almost akin to a faint resemblance of comfort. Such is the force of habit, that we conceive our few feet square of mess room, to possess something of a home character—if that can in any manner be coupled with the name of home, which is, in the world, perhaps the least like it.

Some of us at the foot of a post, some near a window, some against a wall, or even in the centre of the room, with our clothing hung up on every projecting angle, our eatables perched upon all manner of shelves and ingenious contrivances, and our rough little table and chair, we look like so many gregarious Crusoes; a large invoice of poll-parrots from one of the many

Societies at the North, would render this last illusion complete.

In order to lessen the tedium of the winter evenings, recourse is had to all sorts of games, in which the majority participate with great zest. Sometimes it is a ludicrous imitation of a country show, in which figures an elephant represented by throwing a blanket over the shoulders of two officers, or a grotesque female giant, in which one is mounted upon the shoulders of another; these are paraded through the rooms, preceded by torch bearers and a band of *music* performing favorite airs on hair-combs—the whole headed by some comical genius carrying a broom, in the character of an absurd drum-major. At other times a grand cock-fight is inaugurated, in which the two combatants selected, having patiently submitted to that arbitrary process known as "bucking," butt at each other around the ring in fine style, the defeated "rooster" being overset in the most ludicrous manner. Bets are made, and great faith exhibited in the fighting qualities of the several "birds."

Another species of amusement is that barbarous one called "raiding," which consists in that some twenty of the most desperate characters dash through the room, sweeping before them all they meet, oversetting card-tables and chairs, and throwing into confusion everything and everybody that comes in their way. This heathenish practical joke is the terror of the more sedate portion of the community, for the raiders respect nothing and no one, and the just complaints of such as do not relish the rude sport only adds to their zeal and contributes to their merriment. Gymnastic exercises are also much indulged in; an old hickory broom suspended at each end from one of the cross-beams furnishes a trapeze, which although not very safe is perhaps not much more dangerous than a sharp skirmish, or a desperate cavalry charge.

There has been great rejoicing of late in the prison, owing to the arrival of numerous boxes from the north, containing clothing and eatables for the prisoners. There is an almost child-like delight exhibited over these timely bounties from home. An officer with a "box" becomes at once the admired of all admirers, and receives congratulations as hearty as if he had just "married a fortune."

Truly, "men are but children of a larger growth." Shut a man up in a prison, deprive him of his habitual comforts, torture him with hunger, and it is singular how soon he "remounts the river of his years."

There is considerable excitement here about the gubernatorial elections going on at the north in Pennsylvania, Ohio, and Indiana. To-day being the 13th of October, polls have been opened to test the political sentiment of the prison. The excitement waxes high; for several days past there has been stump speaking, there have been torchlight processions, much canvassing, and cheering, and spirited debates as to the issue. The Curtin, and Brough parties are sanguine; Vallandigham stands but a poor chance.

There is quite a crowd at the polls, and considerable challenging and quizzing.

The polls have been closed. The returns show the following results:

PENNSYLVANIA.

Whole number of votes cast	114
For A. G. Curtin, (Union) 95	
" G. W. Woodward, (Democrat) . . . 18	
Scattering 1	
Majority for Curtin	77

OHIO.

Whole number of votes cast 161	
For John Brough, (Union) 160	
" C. L. Vallandigham, (Democrat) . . 0	
Scattering 1	
Majority for Brough	159
Total Union majority	236

This result proves how scarce among us in the prison is the "copperhead" element. Indeed, any one who has been even but for a short time in the Southern Confederacy, learns that the Rebels despise no class of people more heartily than they do their own sympathizers at the North. They shrewdly say that if these "copperheads" are "*for*" them they ought to be there "*with*" them, to help them fight their battles, and to share their privations; and they look with a well-merited scorn upon these prudent patriots who would revolutionize the country from the luxurious precincts of cozy back-parlors, and who seek to disparage and to disgrace, by stealth, that old flag which they have not the courage openly to forsake!

Two officers[*] have lately escaped from the hospital, under rather amusing circumstances. It appears that one of them, who had been a tailor in his pre-military life, offered to make up a uniform coat for one of the Confederate surgeons on duty at the hospital. The unsuspecting surgeon procured the materials, and the "Yankee" kept his word and made the coat; he did not intend it for the surgeon, however, but for himself; for, one bright afternoon,

---

[*] Major Halsted, 132d N. J., and Lieut. Wilson, 1st Md. Cav.

donning the gray garb of the Confederacy, he coolly walked out of the hospital, accompanied by another Federal *patient* also disguised as a rebel, and not only walked out of the door, but all the way down the Peninsula into the Federal lines. He had the admirable impudence to adopt his victim's title as well as his coat, and assuming considerable airs, gave himself out as a Confederate surgeon on duty in the Richmond hospitals!

ON THE CANAL.

"The hole in the Floor."

V.

1863.

November:—Various forms of Melancholy—Confederate Wails—Surgeons and Chaplains—Supplies from the North—The Great Conspiracy.

VARIOUS FORMS OF MELANCHOLY.

WHILE some of the prisoners endeavor by all sorts of ingenious stratagems to divert their minds from the ennui and monotony of captivity, others give up to their sorrows and pine away in the midst of morbid reflections and dismal forebodings. There is a pale, sallow, resurrected-looking youth whom I see wandering like an ill-fed spectre from room to room; he has been a prisoner during many months, and is reduced to the narrowest possible limits of anatomical contraction. He has large eyes which brighten, at times, when you address him kindly or jocosely; but they are eyes which brighten, not with intellectual sunshine, but rather with the weird radiance of moon-light.

This youth has a hobby.—That hobby is, to make his escape from the prison. He dreams of impracticable rope ladders to be manufactured surreptitiously out of blankets, and to be ingeniously concealed from the keen eye of the Inspector,—perhaps of being lowered from the windows in a basket, like Saul from the walls of Damascus. Over his soup, over his coffee, over his stewed apples, over his huckleberries, that one deep and mysterious scheme absorbs all his faculties; at all hours that restless incubus, urged on by an enraged and merciless rider, gallops fiercely to and fro through the bewildering mazes of his brain,— especially during those periods of fearful tedium when he gazes out through the barred windows at the green fields and forests beyond the swift waters of the James.

One stormy night he resolved to carry his long projected plan into execution, by lowering himself from one of the windows. Already his hands resolutely clutched the bars and his foot actually projected beyond the sill, when upon looking more intently at the pavement below to reassure himself before the final spring, he discovered that he was about to alight upon a Confederate hat; now, it so happened that this hat contained a head, and that this head was an indispensable portion of the anatomy of a Confederate sentinel. The lamentable results which would have attended his descent under such adverse circumstances were sufficient to deter him from bringing about so fatal a catastrophe, and he sullenly relinquished his purpose, with a dark and secret vow, the realization of which, if more bloody and terrible than would have been a desperate encounter with a Rebel guard, will not, I dare say, be attended with the same amount of personal peril.

This morbid misanthropy assumes many different forms; it is always melancholy, though variously expressed.

There is a gaunt, sandy-haired individual who may always be seen seated on a *brick*,—why on a brick, I cannot conceive—with his elbows on his knees, and his head between his hands, moaning continually from morning till night, with a pitiable expression of countenance: silent, uncommunicative, and morose. He evidently pets up his grief; I am persuaded that he loves it, and would feel provoked at any one who should cause him to smile. They say he is a Scotchman.

Another eccentric mortal is one whose aberrations follow an entirely different channel. This one has always a black streak somewhere on his face: no wonder,—he is continually in the cook-house, boiling, frying, or stewing something. I do not know when he eats, for I have never seen him yet that he was not cooking: it seems to be his only solace, and his only occupation. I never pass him that some rare and pleasant odor does not greet my olfactories: sometimes of fried eggs, or onions, or nutmeg. He evidently loves to envelope himself in a perpetual atmosphere of culinary fragrances. It is, I dare say, *his* plan, to cook up his melancholy into all sorts of delicious concoctions, and to feed upon it in a substantial and rational manner. I am informed that he is a Frenchman.

Then there is that quiet, reserved, and portly body, who is seldom out of his corner, unless for an evening walk, and who reclines so comfortably in his capacious box-arm-chair, with a huge double-barrelled pipe in his mouth. He envelopes himself in an impenetrable atmosphere of tobacco smoke, puffing it out like a steam-engine, and smacking his lips after every discharge, as though he had just sipped of the exhilarating contents of an invisible glass of Lager. This one *smokes up* his melancholy; he consumes it; he sends it curling upward out of the prison window in huge, serpentine coils of odorous vapor; he puffs out around him a tempestuous little firmament, in the midst of which his incandescent pipe-bowl, like an ominous sun, looms red through the infuriated swirls of stormy smoke-cloud! He smokes, not with ordinary gusto, but with the violence and ferocity of despair; he *must* do it; it is his only hope; take his pipe from him, and in less than twenty-four hours he will be in a strait-jacket in the Insane Asylum; suggest it to him and you will hear him reply: "Gott bewahre! Nicht um die ganze welt! Sie ist mir lieber als das Leben!"

There is yet another: a singularly contradictory specimen of the morbid. He is constantly singing, dancing, or sleeping. His irresistible merriment wrings an echo even from the sober prison walls; he shakes the very bars in the windows, as he leaps about in his jolly dance; he convulses the whole prison with his laughter. He is always ready with a song, a jig, or a joke. And yet I know he is very miserable; I am positively sure that he is racked nearly to death with ennui, weary in mind, and sick at heart. He hails from the Emerald Isle.

There is a great outcry in the Confederacy about the exorbitant prices which have to be paid for articles of first necessity. Truly do they say:

"The question of high prices is, perhaps, the one now most urgent. How are the people—the soldiers —their wives and children to live—how is the Government to get along—with the enormous and increasing prices required for all necessaries? This is a matter which must press upon the heart and mind of every thinking man and lover of the country. The first step towards solving the problem, is to ascertain the chief cause of this depreciation of the value of our money. Extortioners are a curse to our country. As an affair of equity, if prices must advance, all prices should advance simultaneously, and none should receive more justice in this respect than the defenders of the country.—The value of our currency is not fixed and stable, and therefore no change of wages will remedy the injustice, or meet the difficulty. The principal cause of our monetary troubles is the inflation of our currency.—Energy and wisdom in the Government alone can furnish an adequate remedy for the evils of our disordered country."

Lieutenant Skelton of the 17th Iowa, and a fellow patient, escaped yesterday from the Hospital by bribing one of the sentinels. Lieutenant Skelton had been lying in the Hospital a long time, severely wounded.

The Federal surgeons confined here since the suspension of the cartel are, at last, to be sent North. There is great rejoicing among the Faculty in view of their joyous deliverance from thralldom; we join them heartily in their self-congratulation, for there are noble fellows in the number of these ingenious menders of earthen-ware, who go once more into the field to cement together, as best they can, the human pottery cracked in the shock of armies.

The chaplains, detained on either side notwithstanding the non-combatting sanctity of their office, were sent away more than a month ago. Thus deprived of the medical advice of the one class of Doctors, and of the spiritual comfort to be derived from the other, we feel the loss to be a severe one, both to our bodies and our minds. In a *social* point of view we must regret their absence, however much we may philanthropically rejoice at their deliverance from this abnormal little world of ours, in which the body is always ailing and the mind is never at rest.

A number of boats laden with clothing and commissary stores from our Government are lying in the canal, fronting the prison. These are intended to relieve the needy condition of the Federal prisoners here and on Belle Isle. There are also contributions from various Northern Sanitary Commissions, and other charitable Societies; also generous donations from private individuals, and boxes from the families of prisoners.

A monster plan for the deliverance of all the Federal prisoners in Richmond, and for the capture and destruction of the city, has lately come to light. The plan was more or less as follows:

The officers confined in the Libby, headed by the most determined and desperate of their number, were to break out of the prison by force, overpower the sentries, and seize the arms stacked at the Head-quarters of the guard on the opposite corner of the street; the prisoners on Belle Isle, and in the various prisons in Richmond, were then to be liberated, the arsenal seized, and all the insurgents armed; the garrisons in the fortifications having been driven out, or overpowered, the city was to be held. The conspirators were to be aided by numerous Union sympathizers. The time appointed for the explosion of this insurrectionary bomb-shell was the first day of the meeting of the Rebel Congress. Jefferson Davis, and as many of the leading legislators as possible were to be secured, and sent prisoners into our lines.

This movement was to be seconded by a force of cavalry and infantry which was to make a dash upon the Rebel capital from the direction of the Peninsula.

The discovery of this huge plot might have led to serious uneasiness on the part of the Rebel

Government, on the score of future attempts of the same sort; but the fact that not only the whole plan, but even a detailed and "reliable" account, in one of our leading Northern Journals of the *actual occurrence* of these events, while they, as yet, existed only in the visionary minds of the conspirators, must have had the effect of setting the fears of the Rebel authorities completely at rest on the score of such future attempts; the aforesaid newspaper, a co-conspirator, and fully informed of all the most secret plans, would, no doubt, anticipate the actual explosion, and thus afford the Confederacy ample time to guard against the emergency. The first and most vital requisite for the success of conspiracies, is secrecy: a secret, connected with a conspiracy for the capture of Richmond, and shared with a newspaper, might as well have been shared at once with Secretary Benjamin himself.

Notwithstanding the self-complacency of the Richmond authorities after the revelation of this grand conspiracy, it is a historical fact, that a few days ago, several pieces of Confederate cannon were planted near the prison so as to command the streets leading to and from it, and that the guards have been doubled and paraded in unusual numbers before us. Whether by this display of Rebel strength and vigilance, it is intended to intimidate the most desperate, or appeal to the self-preservative instincts of the more timid, I cannot say; but, from what I see and hear around me, the vital points in question among the prisoners, just now, appear to be—the stewing of rations, and the scouring of cook-pots; from which I gather that most of them are of opinion that, under the present unpromising circumstances, it would be far more philosophical to continue to live uncomfortably, than to attempt to die uselessly.

CASTLE THUNDER.

"Our Mess."

VI.

1863.

December:—Shadows—Musical—Christmas—New Year's Eve—A Story about Six Eggs—Another Story.

SHADOWS.

WINTER is upon us, to add new evils to the catalogue of those we already suffer. There is no more sitting at the windows now, in the pleasant, thoughtful twilight, and watching the changes in the sky. The landscape of the James River,—that same little picture set in a window frame and bars, which we somehow never grew weary of looking at—is now cheerless indeed; the leaves have dropped from the trees, and the fields look brown and barren; there is ice on the canal, and patches of early snow on the river-banks; the little green island with the beautiful trees looks dismal and deserted, and the river is muddy, swollen and fretful. Those who love nature had made a great deal of this little picture, uninteresting enough, perhaps, under ordinary circumstances; we had watched the fresh wind whirling the cloud-shadows across it, under the summer sunshine, and blowing the green boughs about, and rippling the surface of the river; we had marked the storm gather above it and break upon it, in the hot days, in showery waterfalls of sparkling cloud-spray; we had seen its glistening, glowing green, shimmering through the last golden gushes of the sunny rain; and we had followed day after day, the evening sunlight as it died behind it, leaving it sad and shadowy, but still lovely, with a pale star above it. There was something to be learned, and much to be remembered by it; for memory wandered on beyond the purple horizon, to loved, familiar places far away, and the keen arrow of thought, piercing the veil which shut them out, went speeding through the far azure to fall at the threshold of a home!

Captivity with a patch of green, and a ray of sunlight to cheer the eye and refresh the heart, now and then, was somehow less hard to bear than now, in the dull and sombre winter days.

They who have never been shut up for months in a gloomy prison-house, can form but a faint idea of the beneficial influences of light upon the human mind. We naturally associate darkness with all that is dread, with all that is sinister, repulsive and unnatural. Light, on the contrary, is typical of all that is good and true, of all that is innocent and happy. Death, ignorance, sorrow, hatred, sin: these are of the shadow. Hope, wisdom, truth, religion, love: these are of the light.

Even the wretched Confederate candle which helps us while away the tedium of these long winter evenings, exercises upon our minds far more important influences than we would be ready, at the first glance, to ascribe to its humble charity of light. Physiologists tell us how much light contributes to the preservation of health, and to the proper development of all forms of life. If it be of so great a value to the body, how infinitely greater must be its value to the mind. I am satisfied that there is less health in the prison since the sun began to shorten his daily pilgrimage, and more gloom in the prison faces since his rays, which used to shoot such glittering golden arrows at us between the window bars, have wearied of their sport and come now among us, quietly and strangely, asif they were merely Distributing Agents for some Celestial Sanitary Commission.

I can remember with what a strange blending of awe, repugnance, and curiosity, I used, when a child, to lift up stones in the dark, damp cellar-corner, and hunt for the pale, bloodless, sickly shoots, which had sprouted there in the darkness, and how I used to drop them quickly again, for they seemed like gravestones with livid, ghastly corpses under them.—Our prison is full of such pale, sickly sprouts, and if the *Diable Boiteux* were to lift the roof off of it, and afford some sunny habitant of the outer world a glimpse into its interior, he might experience something like my childish superstition, and quickly ask the lame gentleman in black to let drop the sarcophagus lid again over this unnatural sepulchre of the living!

The passion for music is quite general in the prison; a tolerable orchestra has been organized, consisting of a violin, banjo, guitar, tambourine, and the bones. They have done much to enliven the gloom of the prison, and invariably attract a large crowd of listeners. They have given several performances imitative of the Ethiopian Minstrels, in the cook-room; these performances are quite creditable to the musical taste of the performers, and are attended by large and enthusiastic audiences,—Notwithstanding the Scotch mist of tobacco smoke which ascends in a perpetual cloud from the inevitable pipes of the Teutonic element of the assemblage, and which reminds one of the gauze curtains in the Midsummer Night's Dream; and notwithstanding the necessarily abortive illumination of the dingy apartment by a tier of suicidal tallow dips; and notwithstanding the fact that the spectator must lug down his own barrel to sit in, or must stand on a dining-table at the risk of breaking his neck, and with the certainty of suffering from a severe attack of the cramp in the legs; and notwithstanding the odor of slops, and the rancid vapors from the cooking stoves, which are apt to transfer the cramp from the calves of the legs to the pit of the stomach;—notwithstanding all these unavoidable collaterals of the Libby Concert Room, the result is beneficial, and merits, and receives, the encouragement of all. The performers have a grand and exciting time preparing their performances—and the spectators while pleasantly away, in listening to their humorous jokes, the tedium of the long evenings.

Captain J. B. Litchfield, 4th Maine Infantry; Captain E. E. Chase, 1st Rhode Island Cavalry, and Captain J. L. Kendall, 1st Massachusetts Infantry, have just been selected to be sent to Saulsbury, North Carolina, sentenced to hard labor during the war, in retaliation for an alleged sentence of the same nature by the Federal authorities.

Major H. White, 67th Pennsylvania Infantry, has also disappeared from our midst, and has been sent to Saulsbury; upon what ground, we cannot conjecture.

Christmas! at that name, what pleasant visions come thronging to the prisoner's mind, visions of home and the hearth,—of mince pies, plum-puddings and bon-bons, of Christmas trees and child-laughter, and pretty little rosy mouths, sweeter for the sugar-plums, puckering into Christmas kisses! What prison-thoughts, that laugh at the rebel bars and bayonets, go traveling by swift air lines, afar off into cozy cottages among the northern snows, and over the wide prairies into western homes; north, south, east and west—over the whole land; fond thoughts, winged with love-lightning!

The north wind comes reeling in fitful gushes through the iron bars, and jingles a sleigh-bell in the prisoner's ear, and puffs in his pale face with a breath suggestively odorous of egg-nog.

Christmas day! a day which was made for smiles, and not for sighs,—for laughter, and not for tears,—for the hearth, and not for the prison. The forms which I pass as I saunter up and down the low, gloomy rooms, are bowed in thought, and their cheeks are pale with surfeit of it; it seems very cruel, but the loving little arms that are felt twining about the neck,—the innocent laughing little faces that *will* peep out of the shadows, with sunbeams in their eyes, —the warm hands which grasp ours in spite of us,—

all these must be thrust aside, and the welling teardrop in the eye must be brushed away, and ... tut tut! what's in a uniform, after all, if the soldier cannot make his brain as thread-bare as its sleeve, nor his heart as hard as its buttons!

There is a group in a dusky corner that I can see from here: some one is playing "Home, sweet home!" on a violin. It is a very dismal affair, this group: the faces are all sad,—no wonder, for the tune is telling them strange, wild things: there are whispering voices in its notes: I see that one by one the figures stroll away, and that they all seem to have discovered something of unusual interest to look at, out of the windows.

I am invited out to-day to a Christmas dinner. Good! There is not much inducement left for phantasmal visitations, after a hearty meal. When I say I am invited *out*, I mean over there in the north-east corner of the room: I shaved my face, and combed my hair, this morning, for the occasion. I am promised a white china plate to eat from!

When I arrive at the north-east corner, I enquire after my host, who is not present. I am informed that he is down in the kitchen, stewing the mutton(!) There he comes, in a violent perspiration, with a skillet in one hand and a tea-pot in the other.

There are four of us,—the dinner is excellent,—I have never tasted a better, even at the *Maison Dorée;* the wine, not very choice, of course,—it is put down on the bill of fare as " Eau de James, couleur de boue."

It is true that the table is made from a box, that the table-cloth is a towel, and that I was requested to bring with me my own fork and spoon; but it is a decidedly *recherché* and ceremonious affair, notwithstanding; my host is polite and elegant to a fault.

After dessert, having stepped over to my "house" for my pipe, which I had forgotten in the excitement of making my toilet (an absence of mind probably due to my having combed my hair,) I return with unexpected celerity, and I find my host, and the two other guests, with their sleeves rolled up to the elbow, scouring the kettles, and washing up the dishes!

So Christmas-day passes away; there are many extra dinners gotten up, and numerous invitations to admired friends. Towards evening, the gloom has in a measure passed off from most of the faces; there is some laughing, and even cracking of jokes. A "ball" has been advertised to take place in the lower east room; an unusual array of tallow candles renders the room as clear as day—a cloudy day, at least; there is a great deal of sport and merriment, after a while, and a great deal of bad dancing; toes are trampled upon with impunity—hats crushed—trowsers torn;—but the violinist scrapes away with supernatural tenacity, and he is the best-natured man in the room, for he is a "fiddler" whom "nobody pays."

At nine o'clock there is a loud cry of "lights out!" from the sentries; the ball breaks up; blankets are spread on the floor; and dancers, spectators, fiddler and all, are soon wrapped in the arms of the Libbyan Morpheus. Many strange visions are beheld; many pleasing dreams experienced; and many fond, familiar faces are photographed in that wondrous *camera obscura* which sleep makes of the dreamer's brain.

It is New Year's Eve. The prison authorities have granted us the privilege of burning candles until midnight: we experience something of the bewilderment of owls,—we have seen nothing clearly after nine P. M., for the last six months.

A group of us are sitting, *à la Turque*, on an outspread blanket: we are waiting to see the New Year in. We have no wine wherewithal to offer up a libation; but we have in a black flask, a very small quantity of Drake's Plantation Bitters, which has been hoarded up for some weeks past to serve on this occasion.

We while away the time by relating anecdotes of

soldier-life. There is in the party an old Hungarian veteran; a genuine old "dog of war," with a copious dash of quaint humor about him. He is telling us *how General Lee got between him and six fresh eggs;* I will let him relate the story himself.

"**On the morning** of the second day of the battle of Gettysburg, I had been ordered to the front by General ———, to ascertain the cause of some scattering discharges of musketry on our right. I rode to the picket line, and having satisfied myself as to the true state of affairs in that direction, I was returning to headquarters with the information I had gathered, when I discovered a small farm-house at a short distance from the road I was following. I had Hans, my old orderly, with me.

"'*Isten neki! Hans*,' said I, placing my hand on my stomach, 'there's a farm-house!'

"'So there is!' ejaculated Hans, placing *his* hand on *his* commissariat.

"I was very hungry. Hans was very hungry, too. We had eaten nothing that day; indeed, we had eaten scarcely any thing for several days, for you may remember what a hasty march we had of it through Virginia and Maryland. 'Hans,' continued I, suggestively, 'that farm-house looks very cozy.'

"'It wouldn't surprise me, sir,' added Hans, tipping his cap to me, 'if you could get a bite of something there, sir.'

"'*Terringettet!* We'll try it!' exclaimed I; for I was of Hans' opinion.

"So we put spurs to our horses, and a few moments afterwards I was dismounting in front of the house.

"The good woman, and a number of little urchins, whom I found there were very much alarmed; the little ones ran away to hide themselves. The woman said, in answer to my queries, that she had not a thing to eat in the house; but I was too hungry to be turned away in that style. I reassured her by stating that I was a Federal officer, (a fact about which she had evidently entertained some misgivings,) and upon my displaying a formidable roll of 'green backs,' she finally acknowledged that she had about six fresh eggs in the larder.

"'Six fresh eggs!' cried I, '*Isten neki!* a feast for the gods! my good woman, I am very hungry. I have eaten nothing to-day. Now, here's the price of the six eggs; have them ready to fry for me in about half an hour, when I will return. On no account allow any one else to get hold of them.'

"I then paid her liberally for the eggs, and mounting my horse, in high glee at the prospect of a glorious meal, I hastened back to headquarters.

"When I arrived there, I found the General mounted; he asked me to accompany him to the front.

"Hans and I exchanged a look of dismay.

"It was of no use; duty before fresh eggs!

"I was never before so much put out in my life. We made a long and tedious reconnoissance; it seemed to me to last an age; for, as you may suppose, I was growing more hungry all the time; I thought we never would start back for headquarters. At last, however, the General, satisfied with his inspection, turned his horse's head in the desired direction.

"Hans and I exchanged a knowing wink, expressive of our supreme satisfaction.

"We had been out several hours, and the cool morning wind had sharpened my appetite to a wonderfully keen edge. Arrived at headquarters, I was about to dart off at once in the direction of my eggs, when the General called to me, saying he wished me to write out some urgent orders. I dismounted with a muttered exclamation which was any thing but complimentary to orders in general, and these in particular; I set myself to work with very bad grace; of course, as

I was in a hurry, I blotted the paper, I spilled the ink, I made mistakes and had to rewrite the orders several times;—no wonder, for I was very hungry, and was thinking of my eggs.

"At last I finished the orders; I was free for a few moments; Hans was holding my horse, ready for me; we leaped into our saddles and dashed at full speed in the direction of our breakfast. I imagined I could already hear those glorious fresh eggs frying and spurting in the hot lard on the kitchen stove,—I could scent their delicious odor as if it were wafted towards me through the kitchen door!

"All at once we heard a discharge of musketry in that direction. A frightful presentiment took possession of me.

"A heavier, louder, and longer discharge followed.

"I shouted to Hans to spur on; I was resolved to resort to any desperate measure rather than go breakfastless that day.

"Suddenly there came a terrific discharge of artillery. It grew louder, and more terrible; peal after peal shook the earth and air; we spurred madly on, and reached the summit of a little eminence on the road: alas! what a sight met our eyes!

"The enemy in tremendous force was pressing toward us; our little farm-house was beyond the advancing columns, half concealed by the smoke.

"The Rebel artillery was between me and my breakfast!

"I will not attempt to describe my feelings at that disheartening spectacle; I only know this, that to this day I feel the blood tingle in my head when any of my fellow-officers begin to relate (as a good joke) around the camp-fire, how General Lee got between me and my six eggs."

We have a hearty laugh over the story, and express it as our unanimous opinion that no doubt General Lee must have enjoyed those six eggs for his breakfast.

"*Isten neki!*" exclaims the emphatic Hungarian, striking the palm of his left hand with his right fist, "I will make it a personal matter with General Lee, when the war is over!"

Another officer relates the following adventure:

"What I am about to relate, occurred last winter during the long period of inaction which preceded the battle of Chancellorsville and the invasion of Pennsylvania by General Lee's Army.

"I was on General ——'s staff, in the Valley of Virginia. We had gone into winter-quarters, and except an occasional rencontre with the guerrillas, but little occurred to break the monotony of our daily duties.

"One day, while visiting the picket line, I noticed a very neat looking cottage about half a mile in front of our advanced line.

"You all know that to a soldier in the field, a house is always an object of peculiar interest: there may be fresh edibles obtainable there,—or quarters, or information, or good water; or there may be a pretty face about the premises,—a thing by no means objectionable, anywhere, and which is well calculated to improve the *morale* of fighting-men.

"Well, I was seized with an irrepressible desire to ride over to this house, and would have yielded to it had I not feared exposing myself to a reprimand for passing unnecessarily beyond the lines. One morning, however, being informed by Captain W—— who was on duty at the picket line, that suspicious sounds, indicative of the presence of cavalry, had been heard the previous night in that direction, I at once gave the affair an air of great importance, and directed the Captain, with a few men, to accompany me to the cottage, that we might ascertain something more positive about the matter. When near the house we placed the men in ambush in a convenient place, and proceeded, the Captain and myself, to take a closer view of the premises. We failed to discover any indications of the recent presence of the enemy; nor did we succeed in attracting any of the inmates to the windows, notwithstanding that we talked in a loud voice, coughed boisterously, and slammed the garden gate with premeditated violence.

"Captain W—— and myself were old and tried friends: we held a short council of war, and arrived at the conclusion that it was our duty to ascertain something about the inmates of this mysterious domicile.

"Acting upon this decision, we mounted the steps of the pretty little verandah, and knocked, in a soldier-like and official manner, at the main door. It was not until the third application of our knuckles, administered *crescendo*, that the door betrayed any symptoms of animation; when it did so, we were not a little disappointed at discovering that its mobility was due to a lank and shrivelled hand, to which was attached an elderly gentleman in a broad-brimmed felt hat and intensely green spectacles.

"We did not, of course, state the real object of our visit; we had recourse to the usual expedient,—an interrogatory as to the possibility of purchasing fresh milk and vegetables. The old gentleman, notwithstanding his apparent gentility, was so cold in his manner, and so crusty in his replies, that the necessity of beating an awkward and precipitate retreat became obviously imperative. We were on the point of doing so, when I observed one of the parlor curtains drawn gently aside, and a most angelic female face peep out modestly at us.

"Had I been suddenly struck in the pit of the stomach by a thirty-two pound solid shot, I could not have experienced a more violent shock!

"I was always a great *ladies' man;* indeed, to be candid, that is my weak point, and I can trace back nearly every casualty and *contretemps* of my life to my experiences with the fair sex. Captain W——, who had been also just attacked in *his* weak point, stood like myself, staring stupidly at the lovely visitation in the parlor window, and, in all human probability, neither one of us would ever have taken any further notice of the old gentleman, had not he also turned toward it, and ordered back the fair vision with an authoritative wave of his bony and wrinkled hand.

"I felt as though I could, at that moment, have condensed the old fellow, spectacles and all, into the crown of his hat, had not so insane a purpose been checked by the timely reflection that he might be the legitimate author of that beautiful creation, and that so sanguinary a proceeding might be calculated to impair my prospects of winning her good graces. I, therefore, changed from an offensive, rather to a defensive system of tactics. All my efforts in that direction, however, proved futile, and when I left, a quarter of an hour later, the old porcupine was as bristling and forbidding as ever.

"On our way back to our lines, not a word with reference to the exquisite creature we had beheld, passed between W—— and myself. You can readily surmise how it was: we were already rivals. Unfortunately for me, W—— was remarkably handsome, very clever, and shrewd as a fox.

"I could not, during several days, drive away that beautiful vision from my brain; it haunted me constantly; it pursued me night and day; as I stood time after time, gazing at the pretty cottage from our lines, I often imagined I could distinguish a white handkerchief waved to and fro among the evergreens which fenced the little garden, and more than once, on such occasions, I had *Wistar's Lozenges* recommended to me as an infallible specific for a severe cold in the head.

"I dreamed of that fatal beauty every night. Sometimes I would dream that the sky was a huge parlor window, and that between two curtains of fleecy cloud, suddenly parted by a gush of wind, her blushing face looked out, and smiled upon me: some mornings this pleasant hallucination would be due to the sun, which as it rose shone full in my face,—or it would be Joe, my colored boy, who would suddenly throw open the tent flaps to call me to breakfast.

"It was not long before I found an excuse for going again to the cottage. This time I did not wait to be invited into the house; the fair angel was in the parlor; I had given my name to the old gentleman; he could not do less than to say: 'Captain ——, my daughter, sir.' Thus was I rewarded with her acquaintance for my consummate impudence. What a lucky dog I thought myself, to be sure! I did not feel quite so well satisfied, however, when during our pleasant little chat, she mentioned quite familiarly, the name of Captain W——. So, so, thought I, that rascal has forestalled me!

"I will not weary you with a detailed account of all the cunning stratagems I had recourse to, in order to advance my suit; suffice it to say that I seemed to have made a most decided impression upon the lovely girl,—at least, so my vanity interpreted her tender manner, and her encouraging smiles. One fact I *was* confident of: I had ousted W——, and had driven him completely from the field. That painful and awkward coolness which arises between the best friends when there is a contest between them for a woman's heart, had sprung up between us; we were quite shy of each other; we never alluded, even distantly, to the pretty cottage or the precious jewel it contained.

"Well, the affair continued to prosper in the most charming manner for me; I had, now and then, a stolen interview with my lovely tormentor, in which I must admit, in justice to her modesty, that she always compelled me to speak to her from the opposite side of the hedge. I deemed her a model of angelic purity and feminine reserve, and these precious qualities of course added a keener zest to my tender passion. After a time, however, I insisted on a clandestine interview *without* a hedge; she objected emphatically, but tenderly; I pressed my advantage, and opened every battery I could bring into position,— she wavered,—I charged with all my cavalry, and, after a desperate resistance, she finally consented to grant me an interview, such as I solicited. This meeting was to take place in the parlor, the following evening.

"There is no hedge in the parlor, dreamed I, as I returned to our lines; I will propose to her, and who knows, after the war, what may come of it. It was so romantic to be loved by a beautiful enemy (for she was the rankest kind of 'Secesh'); and the personal peril of these secret interviews,—it was so exciting and exhilarating!

"The day following was one, to me, of the greatest nervous agitation; the hours seemed days—the day a week. I met W—— early in the evening; he evidently observed my nervous condition, and it seemed to render him quite nervous also—poor fellow! I pitied him; it was a shame to 'cut him out;' but how could *I* help it? Are we to be expected to control the hurricane blasts of love? Are its volcanic fires to be extinguished with a mouthful of water? Are its seething whirlpools to be stilled by a drop of sweet oil? Are its alpine avalanches to be staid with the toe of one's boot? Of *course* not! Oh, had he only suspected what happiness awaited me that night! I could not repress a commiserative smile. He smiled too (of course it was in defiance).

"At last, night came—a beautiful night! There was no moon, to be sure,—but then, after all, moonlight is *so* hackneyed; there were, instead, innumerable stars—delicious, poetical stars, so like an enchanted shower of silver rain, spell-bound in space!

"I had my confidential orderly with me; I ambushed him in a wood near the cottage, and proceeded alone, as was my wont. How fast my heart throbbed as I opened the garden gate! It might be all a dream! I dreaded, every moment, that my boy Joe would throw open my tent and wake me up for breakfast! Might she not have repented her promise? I was soon convinced of the fallacy of this last dire suspicion, for I descried her graceful form enveloped in a shawl, leaning in the half-darkness, out of the parlor window; she saw me approach, and came, softly, to open the door for me. There was a little vestibule, through which it was necessary to pass in order to reach the parlor; she whispered, 'Follow me!' *Follow her*—follow that angel form—that celestial voice—yes! to the very end of the universe would I have followed her!

"It was very dark, but I guided my steps by the rustle of her gown; she opened the parlor door—I entered after her—I heard the key turn in the lock. 'Shade of Venus!' thought I, 'this is more than my most sanguine anticipations could have led me to hope for!'

"'Where are you?' I whispered, with a tremulous and excited accent, natural enough under such peculiar circumstances.

"She returned no answer.

"I reached out for her with my hands.

"I touched the door.

"She was gone!

"The door was locked—*on the outside!*

"'Zounds!' I exclaimed, growing apprehensive. 'What can this mean? Perhaps she only wishes to make sure that I shall not be disturbed by the parent in spectacles, while she perfects the arrangements for our interview.'

"I waited patiently for awhile; finally, I heard her step approaching the door again; I had been listening, with my ear to the key-hole.

"She unlocked the door.

"Oh! what a mysterious thrill of happiness shot through my heart.

"I drew back, that my previous apprehensions might not be suspected.

"She entered: I heard her step on the carpet.

"The door was locked again.

"This was glorious!

"'Dearest' I whispered tenderly 'at last!'

"I stretched forth my hand to clasp her own.

"I did clasp it.

"But it was not her's!

"It was a man's! Oh! horror! A rough, bony, hairy hand.

"'What does this mean' I exclaimed indignantly, 'Who are you, sir?'

"'The deuce!' answered the familiar voice of Captain W——.

"'Is that *you*?'

"If I had accidentally stepped on a torpedo I could not have been more completely blown up!

"'What brings *you* here,' I demanded imperatively, as soon as I had collected the exploded fragments of myself.

"'My dear fellow,' whispered he, 'I fear we have been most confoundedly sold.'

"'What? I shivered out 'a trap?'

"'A trap,' shivered he.

"We were not long permitted to indulge in our gloomy vaticinations. After the lapse of a few moments, a stream of light suddenly shot through the key-hole of another door at the farther end of the room, and the old gentleman in the green spectacles entered, holding a candle, and followed by a dozen men in gray coats, armed to the teeth, and headed by a ferocious-looking officer.

"The whole frightful truth flashed upon us in an instant.

"We had been betrayed!

"The officer advanced towards us pistol in hand.

"'Gentlemen,' he said, levelling his weapon, 'you are my prisoners!'"

"For my part, I was so completely stupefied and thunderstruck by the startling occurrences of the last ten minutes that I candidly believe I would have surrendered unconditionally to the old gentleman, had he come all alone, and simply armed with a broomstick!

"As we were being led out, I caught a last glimpse of a charming family group: my beautiful angel, laughing to kill herself, was pressed in the arms of the ferocious officer, who was calling her his darling *wife!* (Hang the fellow!)—The old gentleman was looking after us, holding the candle above his head, with the first, last, and only smile I had ever yet seen upon his crabbed, surly, and frigid physiognomy!

"Our feelings, as we mounted doggedly behind two of the Rebel troopers, I will not attempt to convey: shame, at the consequences of our dishonorable capture,—indignation at the base treachery of that beautiful fiend, tortured us into a vortex of agony which baffles all description. W—— and myself beheld in our common fate, a merited punishment for our common folly.

"But, fortunately, this awkward affair was not destined to terminate as fatally for our reputation as we at first had reason to expect.

"The force which guarded us was small; their

horses, too, were evidently much jaded; my orderly had in all likelihood heard, and suspected, what was going on; we might yet be rescued.

"So, indeed, it happened. We had not travelled far before the sound of horses at full gallop was heard behind us. Our captors quickened their own pace in proportion.

"Ere long our pursuers had caught up with us, and a brisk skirmish ensued, during the confusion and excitement of which, W—— and myself contrived to make our escape.

"The full history of our affair did not become generally known; such encounters with Rebel guerrillas were of too frequent occurrence to excite much attention. Those who *did* learn the true history of it, however, gave us no rest for a long time afterwards, and many a joke was cracked at our expense.

"W—— and I, became better friends than ever. Neither of us ever went near that cottage again, nor did we ever after meet with any of its occupants; indeed, a short time after our adventure, our forces moved up the valley to a new position—a change of locality upon which we congratulated ourselves heartily.

"We had been taught a salutary lesson; the moral of it is this:

"A Federal may sometimes, under peculiar circumstances, trust a Rebel man,—but a Rebel *woman*, never!"

As he delivered himself of this excellent maxim, the narrator winked his right eye with an emphasis which must have caused a mysterious thrill to curdle the heart of every rebellious female in the Confederacy.

A RATION OF CORN BREAD.

VII.

1864.

January:—New Year's Day—Speculative and Retrospective—Lugubrious—Escapes from the Prison—Belle Isle.

NEW YEAR'S DAY.

"TWELVE o'clock! Post No. 1—all's well!" suddenly breaks upon the stillness of the night.

The New Year is in!

Simultaneously a voice in the prison begins to sing *The Star-Spangled Banner;* it is taken up, voice after voice, until the swelling strain rises from every room in the building, and floats out upon the midnight air, and up to the starry sky, in one grand chorus of enthusiastic voices!

After this follows *Auld Lang Syne.*

That over, there follows such a noise of cheers, yells, clattering of tin-ware, shouts of "Happy New Year!" and such a hideous concatenation of demoniacal sounds, as might with considerable reason have been expected to frighten the new year from coming into the prison until next day.

New Year's day is spent much in the same manner

as Christmas; there are extra dinners, and a great deal of extra noise. In the evening there is a "Grand Ball" in the kitchen. The musicians are mounted on a table placed against the wall; they discourse tolerable music from a tambourine, violin, banjo, and bones; there is a great crowd; with one exception, all are men—that one is a man also, but disguised into a ludicrous representation of a negro woman—well blacked up, and with a wreath of flowers on her (his) head,—this Ethiopian female is a First Lieutenant of Regulars! The pseudo-feminine is accompanied by a comical representation of a colored beau; they are the great centre of attraction, and they open the Ball in fine style.

What a sight!—to see several hundred men dancing together at this inhuman, unnatural Ball, in the gloomy cook-room of a prison! I say *gloomy* with all due deference to the weak-eyed, near-sighted, tallow-dips, which seem to understand, and to feel, the absurdity of their position, and are flickering away, and guttering down, as though making all haste to use themselves up as soon as possible.

Among these heathenish dancers, there are many, —young men of the fashionable stamp,—who whilom sported dress coats and lemon-colored kids at ceremonious parties in aristocratic parlors!

Oh, what base uses we may come to! To think of placing one's arm around, and gracefully seizing the hand of, some rough, **hairy Hoosier**, or some porpoisine "gun-boat," and whirling them through that exhilarating maze, reserved only for delicious contact with slender waists and soft, **white hands**. O, shade of Terpsichore!

When the Ball is over, the frightful serenade of the previous night is again inaugurated. Are these men mad? What a deafening clatter of tin-ware! What insane yells! What stamping, and leaping, and shouting! **I am** informed that it is a War Dance. If so, the Sioux and Camanches are utterly outdone!

On the floor below, two sane men are near the termination of a highly interesting game of chess; there is a great thumping and clattering of feet on the floor over-head, but it does not seem to interfere with the labor of those mental engines, whose potent energies are absorbed in the profound tactics of the chess-board; a large circle of intelligent spectators are intent upon the next move, which must be decisive. Black's hand is outstretched, tremulous with ill-controlled excitement: White turns pale, for those nervous outstretched fingers clutch a portentous black rook, and in another instant the white king will be mated. . . . **When lo!** from the ceiling overhead, where it was hung, down comes a huge ham, and drops like a bomb-shell into the very midst of the contending hosts! The pieces are scattered right and left; the board, and the rickety table on which it stood, are overset; and the black and the white general both spring to their feet with a cry of horror, which is only drowned in shouts of the heartiest laughter from the bystanders. The *war-dance* was still going on overhead, and a gigantic Indian warrior having leaped five feet into the air, and come down directly above the suspended ham, had jarred it from the nail on which it hung, and had thus ruined the most brilliant game of chess ever played in the prison!

Much in the same style ends the celebration of the New Year's advent.

The horizon of the future is bright with rumors of "exchange;" there is a frightful epidemic of that alarming malady known as "Exchange on the brain;" some are sanguine; most are hopeful; and all are anxious for the arrival of that happy day of liberation which has been looked forward to so long in vain. Should the ensuing month bring with it that glorious millenium, it will not have been an empty hope which prompted us all to-day to wish one another "A happy New Year!"

In this prison-life of ours, so curiously interwoven are the sublime and the ridiculous, the pathetic and the humorous, that it is no easy task to separate the one from the other. There are hours of profound melancholy, and moments of reckless *sans-souci*.

Most of the prisoners, being soldiers only pro tem., have at variance within them two distinct elements of feeling : one springing from their habitual, and the other from their temporary mode of life ; one springs from peaceful associations with the seclusion of home, or the luxury or business activity of city life,—the other from the more recent influences of the camp and the battle-field. These incongruous elements are in constant antagonism. One moment it is the soldier, improvident of the future, reckless of the present, laughing at discomfort and privation, and merry in the midst of suffering ; then again it is the pacific citizen, complaining of misfortune, sighing for home, dreaming of seclusion and peace, yielding to despondency and to sorrow. And this is perhaps fortunate—for thus, at least, there is less danger that the prisoner shall become either a prodigal with the one element, or a miser with the other.

Most people are apt, when left continually to their own thoughts, to indulge in a sort of *post-mortem* examination of their previous life; to dissect that portion of their personal history, which is seldom anatomized without arriving at the conclusion that our present misfortunes are, in nearly all cases, due to some radical error in our own record.

How many have, at some time, sighed to themselves: *Alas! my life has been a failure!*

Misfortune renders some men reckless; they lash the helm—take in sail—and scud away under bare poles over the tempestuous ocean of the world. Others, on the contrary, become cautious through adversity and wise through failure, and such, retracing in their leisure hours their path of life, go back and question the sorrowful spectres of perished hopes, which haunt the crowded grave-yards of the past; they draw from its cerements the cold, wan reality of by-gone years; they cut into the body of their blighted, dead past-life, and seek to learn of what disease it died. This is rational,—it is instructive,—it is courageous; unfortunately, it is not agreeable. Much pleasanter it is, amid the platitudes of our daily existence, to lean toward the amenities, rather than the duties, of thought. Better, we deem, to light anew about the corpse of the dead Past the halo of a specious existence; to enwreathe the torn hair with blossoms,—to tinge the livid cheek with the purple flush of health,—to enkindle the glazed eyes with eloquent lustre,—to breathe into the pallid lips the wonted echoes of a familiar voice which may discourse to us pleasantly of long departed joys, and of old, happy hours. There is indeed, a sort of piteous consolation in doing this; it is like the mournful solace sought by those who, having lost some being near and dear to them, love to plant the honored grave with flowers.

It is this inward self which is all his own, that the prison-leisure leads the speculative captive to dissect and to analyze. He is allowed ample time for thought. After a long voyage with memory over the ocean of the past, he returns to the present with a better heart, and endeavors from the new-kindled stars which have risen above the vapory horizon of his prison-life, to cast the horoscope of a wiser future. He has held his post-mortem examination, and in all likelihood, has not failed to discover the nature of the disease.

Prisons, like death-beds, are fertile in repentances; like the regions of Avernus they are paved with good resolutions: fortunately they neither resemble the former in their brevity of duration, nor the latter in their eternity of time,—so that the prison-repentance may be genuine if enduring, and the good resolves fruitful of good if unbroken. It is, indeed, a pity that the fair promises we make to ourselves in captivity, are so apt to be cast aside unfulfilled when we are once free.

But the hour of retrospect and self-humiliation must come for all, sooner or later. Even the scoffer who has journeyed over the path of a long life with his back to Heaven, will turn, as he dies, and take one step towards it!

Glorious and beautiful is the Shakespearean philosophy which teaches us to see good in everything; verily, there are books in the prison bars—and sermons in the prison stones.

Every afternoon I notice in the street, beneath my window, a group of ill-clad juvenile beggars, of both sexes. They hold up their red little hands to us, as they stand there shivering in the cold. We throw to them spare fragments of corn bread, and occasionally a macerated ham bone, which they scramble for greedily, to carry home with them.

There is a loyal, patriotic, and attenuated old cow, who also comes regularly every day to munch at the edible bits and scraps thrown out to her from our windows. When she fails to attract our attention, she shakes her head impatiently, and jingles the bell at her neck, gazing wistfully up at the barred windows.

So it is: these children, who are innocent and hungry—this **poor** beast, who is neglected and starved—these are the only inhabitants of the Confederate Capital, who dare openly to acknowledge their misery, and to show their attachment to the Yankee barbarians, who, wretched and hungry enough themselves, Heaven knows! are yet ready to share even with them the meagre rations on which they are compelled to subsist.

The extinction of the last hope of an exchange of prisoners—at least within a reasonable time, has had the effect of depressing our spirits to an extent truly deplorable. The usual games and pastimes are abandoned; even those villainous nocturnal catechizers, generally impervious to the most grievous calamities, have sunk into a condition of despondency which would be almost gratifying, were it only limited to their own number.

To add to this doleful aspect of affairs, no boxes from home have been distributed among us for several weeks,—so that the majority of us are subsisting chiefly on corn cake, tobacco smoke, and the recollections of former prosperity,—the latter, a species of retrospective diet which makes a capital *bonne bouche* for a post-prandial chit-chat under straitened circumstances, but which, unfortunately, is not possessed of very nutritious qualities. Hence, we are daily becoming more and more depressed, physically as well as mentally,—a depression, which if not checked in its alarming rapidity, will before long bring about a state of collapse, and will probably lead to a series of "special exchanges" into the lines of that bourne from which no Libby traveller ever returns.

I must admit that it requires a great deal of that kind of philosophical *sang froid* so characteristic of the nobles during the French Revolution, who joked and laughed in the tumbrils which conveyed them to the guillotine, to treat so serious a calamity in a manner so trivial. But, as I have been solicited by my fellow-prisoners to compose a readable book of our prison experiences, and as I am inclined to believe that the few who will ever get out of this modern Bastile (there is, *in parenthesis*, a strong anatomical probability, at present, that the author himself will never get out to publish it,) will be like all men who have been prisoners, and like many philosophers who have not, that is—disposed to laugh, rather than to weep over departed evils, I, therefore, take it for granted that I am pursuing the course most in accordance with their wishes. It has been wisely suggested that "To be great, is to be unhappy!" Oh!—if it be requisite to lift one's mental energies from the stagnating platitudes of prison existence, up to the empyreal sublimities of authorship,—if it be necessary to struggle through the torpid vapors of a lugubrious "stale, flat and unprofitable" life, up to the dignities and responsibilities of literary composition,—if Rabelais did not express the truth when he asserted that a body emasculated by famine, and tortured by disease and privation, is incapable of furnishing the intellect which tenants it, with noble and excellent thoughts; if it be absolutely essential to laugh when one feels like crying,—to smile when one would frown,—to write, when one is languid and torpid, on meagre fragments of unsized paper, mutilated fly-leaves of books, and greasy covers of cheap publications, with a fork-pointed pen,—to answer roll-call precisely at the culminating period of a pathetic and intricate passage,—to hasten down to the kitchen in order to concoct an indigestible dinner, and to have your pot boiling over on the stove and your very best ideas boiling over in your brain,—to have hickory brooms inserted unceremoniously between your literary legs at sweeping hours, and the floor washed, and filthy water dashed about in insane and perilous cataracts under your literary nose, on scrubbing days,—if, I groan, it be requisite to endure all this, pending the composition of a readable book of prison experiences,—Oh, then, that this wise saying might be for once reversed, and that it might prove equally true that "To be unhappy, is to be great!"

But to return: Seven mortal days and nights with nothing to eat but stale corn cake, and nothing to drink but cold hydrant water, would, I dare say, have made one of those Revolutionary aristocrats as brisk as a grass-hopper and as merry as a cricket! The result, in our case, is by no means so gratifying; for, our prison presents, just now, not so much the lively prospect of a clover field as of some antiquated museum, in which a rare collection of Egyptian mummies might, by means of a necromantic spell, have been suddenly recalled into existence.

I could not repress a ghastly smile this morning as I sat observing a mess of four, whose breakfast consisted simply of a very small quantity of very weak coffee, and who, with all the gravity of Puritans, employed the time they would, under more favorable circumstances have devoted to eating, in singing "Glory, glory hallelujah!"

Except during the first three weeks following our

arrival here, we have never been reduced to so wretched a condition, with regard to provisions, as we are at present. Empty shelves and empty boxes, meet the eye every where; the pegs which whilom displayed juicy hams and savory tongues, now support only their meagre carcasses, which look, as they pend there, like the shrivelled remains of so many vile criminals hung for piracy.

It is a well-known fact, that those who perish from starvation behold, amid their expiring agonies, visions of superb banquets, tables loaded with the most succulent viands and the choicest and most delicious confections, which, Tantalus-like, they may gaze upon, but cannot reach. I know not if what we are experiencing of the same sort at present, be a premonitory symptom—but it certainly is the prevailing affliction among us. Ah, yes! Miss Leslie's Cookery Book reads like a novel!

This month has been among the most eventful of our prison history.

Its advent was made joyful by the unusually promising aspect of the exchange question, and although the sanguine hopes entertained of its speedy adjustment, and our liberation, were doomed to experience a sudden and unexpected demise, leaving us more gloomy and disheartened than ever, yet, its exit has been attended by a thrill of excitement so unusual as to be almost unprecedented.

The Libby has been, I believe, always considered the safest military prison in the Confederacy; its isolated position, and the vigilance of its commanding officer, **Major Turner**, having entitled it to high encomiums in this regard. If it be true that love laughs at bolts, when its object is a woman—captivity, unfortunately, cannot always indulge its risibility at the expense of bars, even though its object be liberty—one quite as worthy of the affections. A prisoner, if he deserve the name, is always more or less occupied with the idea of making his escape; he becomes a plotter, in spite of his scruples; he forms a thousand plans in his mind, all of which begin by appearing more feasible, and almost invariably end by being considered more impossible, than they really are; the strength and resistance of bars are accurately calculated; the pregnability of walls cautiously and satisfactorily tested; the elevation of windows from the street shrewdly estimated; the vigilance or carelessness of sentries cautiously observed, and their peculiar habits and propensities systematically analyzed. All these preliminary facts having been properly weighed in the balance, the plan is matured, and the opportunity for carrying it into effect is patiently awaited. But, as it happens with those schemes in life which depend for their success more upon accidental and fortuitous contingencies than upon natural and preconceived events, that very opportunity which is the last requisite on the list calculated upon by the schemist, is also the chief one in importance. Without it the shrewdest and best matured plans are destined to fail. Opportunities have changed, at times, the destinies of whole nations.

It happens that the prisoner seldom finds an opportunity ready for him when he could take advantage of it, and quite often it presents itself when he cannot. Now, some officers in the Libby having, notwithstanding the vigilant eye of Major Turner and the fidelity of his guards, discovered some flaws in his precautions for the safe-keeping of his prisoners, arranged their plans accordingly—they were ready for the opportunity precisely at the critical moment when it was ready for them, and five in number, they coolly walked out of the prison one fine afternoon. The first flaw was this: that visitors, mostly citizens of Richmond, were permitted to enter the prison and to leave it without being challenged by the sentries. The next flaw was, that when the invalid officers attended "sick call," every morning, they passed through the same door on their way to the doctor's office, through which these visitors passed in and out unmolested. It was no difficult matter for them to attire themselves in citizen's clothing, or like workmen, or Rebel soldiers, and to avail themselves of this door as a means of exit, not toward the doctor's office, but up the nearest street into the city.

Had not this successful trick been discovered in time, no doubt every man in the prison would have eventually converted himself pro tem. into a fine old Virginia gentleman, or belligerent Butternut, and some pleasant morning the visitors who walked out of it would have been far more numerous than the visitors who walked into it. The consummate impudence of this trick was its most admirable feature,—indeed, it was the true key to its success.

These escapes have been productive of much merriment in the prison, and of joy at the liberation of these, our quondam fellow-sufferers. To be sure, they have still to reach the Federal lines in safety, an undertaking by no means easy, when we consider that the whole Confederacy is indeed a sort of huge Military Penitentiary.*

---

* Captain J. F. Porter is the only one who has succeeded in reaching the Union lines. Major Bates, 80th Illinois, Lieutenant King, 3d Ohio, Lieutenant Cupp, 167th Pennsylvania, and Lieutenant Carothers, 3d Ohio, have been recaptured.

Two more of our number have been sent to Saulsbury, North Carolina, to remain at hard labor during the war, carrying a *ball and chain*. This is also done upon the plea of retaliation. They are Captain Ives, 10th Massachusetts, and Captain J. E. B. Reed, 51st Indiana.

Belle Isle, where some 6,000 Federal prisoners, enlisted men, are confined, is beautifully situated in a bend of the James River, about half a mile above Richmond. In the summer season, it is a delightful spot, and was much frequented, previous to its use as a prison, by pic-nic and other pleasure parties from the city.

The river, which is here very swift of current and broken into innumerable cascades, is full of fantastic groups of rocks, and islets covered with luxuriant foliage, among which it dashes, white with sparkling foam.

The island, which contains some thirty or forty acres of superficial extent, rises, at the lower extremity into a gentle, sandy elevation: upon this is situated the camp for prisoners, occupying a space of about four acres. The upper extremity of the Island is bold and precipitous, rising abruptly into a rocky bluff, crowned by an earth-work which commands the river up-stream.

The view both up and down the river, from the summit of this bluff, is very fine. Looking up-stream the river is seen winding down between hilly banks of cultivated land and luxuriant foliage, its numberless little cascades flashing among the rock-islets; on the right bank are some earthworks commanding the approaches to Richmond in that direction; on the left bank is the cemetery, where the tomb of President Monroe is just discovered among the pines, and below, on the edge of the river are the Water Works which supply the city.

Looking from the bluff down-stream you have a full view of Richmond, with the Capital crowning the highest eminence; on its left the State Penitentiary with its castellated turrets; below it the Tredegar Works, and on your extreme right, Manchester, a village opposite Richmond, on the right bank of the James.

Between Belle Isle and the city, three long bridges span the river, almost shrouded in the rich foliage of the banks and of numerous picturesque islets.

Immediately below you is the prisoners' camp, divided into two sections, each surrounded by a ditch and breastwork,—looking like a crowded, walled, little city of Sibley tents; at the very extremity of the point is a leaning flag-staff from which float the white field and red cross of Rebeldom; on the right bank of the islands are a few brick and frame houses, the only buildings on it; on the left of you, at the foot of the bluff, is the prisoners' grave-yard. This graveyard contains ninety-seven graves; at the head of each is a wooden head-board neatly lettered, with the name, rank, and regiment, and date of decease of the occupant. The oldest grave dates back to June, 1863. The day upon which most deaths occurred was the 5th of January, 1864, on which day four new graves were added.* The grave-yard is located on a slightly elevated bank, close to the edge of the river, which as it rushes past among the rocks, ceaselessly chaunts a mournful requiem over the hapless tenants of that lonely spot.

Lieutenant Bossieux, a Virginian, is in command at Belle Isle: he is a humane and courteous officer.

The sufferings of the Federal prisoners on Belle Isle are severe indeed. The rigors of an unusually cold winter, and the precarious and meagre commissariat of the Confederacy, have at times rendered these sufferings terrible in the extreme. I have been assured by the prisoners themselves that the com-

---

* This refers to deaths which occurred on *the island*,—the sick were regularly sent to the hospitals in Richmond.

manding officer has ever done all in *his* power to render their imprisonment supportable.

There is a bakery on the island for the use of the prisoners and garrison, as also a sutler.

Many attempts to escape, some of them successful, have been made at different times by the prisoners. Among the graves in the lonely little graveyard, is one which shows by the inscription on the head-board, that its tenant was drowned while attempting to swim across the river to the opposite shore; having one day managed to elude the vigilance of the guard, he had secreted himself until night, when he endeavored to swim the stream, but was drowned among its whirls and eddies. His lifeless body was discovered on the following day, caught in a fish-trap in which it had become entangled.

The small-pox has broken out among us. Here and at Belle Isle its ravages have been much mitigated, but at Danville it has made frightful havoc among the Federal prisoners, hundreds having been already *carted* (I use the Rebel expression) to the grave-yards, and it is probable that many more, both there and here, are destined to fall victims to this loathsome and pestilential malady. This frightful accessory alone was needed to complete the sadness of a picture already gloomy and repulsive enough.

But these horrors have not been endured by men alone. Lately, a woman disguised as a soldier, was discovered among the prisoners on Belle Isle. She had for more than a month endured the terrors of a situation which needs no comment, and had preserved her incognito unsuspected until compelled by sickness to repair to the hospital, where she confessed her true sex. She is a young girl of seventeen or eighteen years of age, of prepossessing appearance, and modest and reserved demeanor. She persistently refused to throw any light upon her previous history, or to reveal the motive which had induced her to adopt the garb and the calling of a soldier. She had served during more than a year in a cavalry regiment in the West, when made a prisoner. She had probably followed to the field some patriotic lover, or adventurous spouse. When these facts became known to us in the Libby, a sum was at once contributed by the officers, sufficient to purchase the female soldier garments suitable to her sex, wherewith she might present a more becoming appearance on her return to the Union lines.

VIII.
1864.

February:—A SERMON FROM A CANDLE—THE PRISON WORLD—CROWDED CONDITION OF THE PRISON—COOKING EXPERIENCES—LETTERS—THE GRAND ESCAPADE.

A SERMON FROM A CANDLE.

IT is a wondrously pleasant thing to sit, on a winter evening, in one's comfortable room, leaning lazily back in a cushioned arm-chair, one's feet propped up by the burnished fender and warmed by the glow of the crackling anthracite. The wind howls without, and drives the cutting sleet against the window panes, with a sound which serves marvellously to increase our sense of comfort, and our store of thankfulness. Ah, how pleasantly we ruminate then, as we watch the gleaming jets of ruby and of azure darting and winding among the glowing coals! Those may, indeed, be grateful and pleasing thoughts of happy morning hours, fresh and green, islanded here and there along the downward current of life's river; of present noon-day hopes sailing calmly onward to peaceful havens; of a tranquil, bright horizon, gleaming down the stream, under an evening sky of violet and of gold!

But, alas! it is quite another affair to sit in your stiff-backed, hard-seated flour-barrel-arm-chair, in a cheerless prison, with the winter wind blowing polar needles in your face through the paneless, shutterless windows,—your hat slouched down on the windward side of your head for a shield,—and to behold around you your shivering fellow-prisoners, blowing their fingers to keep them warm, and all muffled up in their gray blankets, as if they were so many uneasy Rebel ghosts stalking about in Confederate winding-sheets; to have no letters to write, and no book to read, and to sit there staring at your one yellow Confederate tallow candle, stuck in an impracticable cake of corn bread for a candle-stick—staring at it as though you might, by some hitherto unsuspected optical process, extract, for your own bodily comfort, the meagre caloric of its flickering flame,—then from the candle passing your eye to the candle-stick, and staring at that, as though you were speculating upon the frightful probability of having to devour it for your breakfast to-morrow, tallow-drippings and all.

This, I repeat, is quite another case, and the ruminations which occupy your brain are of a correspondingly diverse character. It is all very well to recollect that you once read a beautiful and instructive lecture by Doctor Farraday on the wonderful chemical processes which take place in a burning candle; it may have interested you hugely at the time to read about oxygen and hydrogen, and the many extraordinary antics which these gases play in the blaze of your tallow-dip, and how if it were not for the nitrogen in the air, it would burn itself up in a snap of your fingers. Your thoughts do not flow in this channel just now—unless, indeed, the alarming rapidity with which your candle uses itself up, notwithstanding the charitable assistance of the nitrogen, should suggest the melancholy reflection that this distressed, bilious-looking taper has cost you the round sum of one dollar!

Your thoughts are resolutely cast in the rigid mould of that gloomy philosophy which teaches you, not so much to endeavor to fly from the evils which beset you, but rather to grapple with them, and trample them under foot. But this admirable system of ethics it is not always easy to put into practice; so you continue to stare at your candle, and you stare so intensely and so long, that if you are a hypochondriac (and of course you *are* one) you may readily be led into the suicidal hallucination that you also are made of tallow, and have a burning wick protruding from the top of your head, and that, after all, you are only two candles staring blankly at one another, and watching each other melt away, inch by inch, with a sort of silent, demoniacal satisfaction!

Finally, you arrive at one, and only one conclusion, which is, that if there be any one thing in this world more utterly unsatisfactory than any other, it is to be a prisoner of war. He who is imprisoned for the commission of a crime, has at least the consolation of knowing that he deserves the punishment he suffers. But the idea of being shut up in a dreary and loathsome tomb, for weeks and months—to be tortured, and pinched, and starved—merely for serving your country, and endeavoring, through it, to serve humanity! Had you failed to answer at your country's call, such tortures might be fully merited. Stop! you must call your moral ethics here to your aid, for you feel that the burning wick in your head is playing the deuce with your cerebral tallow. You moralize for a while, and you finally arrive at the conclusion, (you could not very well arrive at any other,) that it is *all for the best*. Now, with Portia you exclaim:

> "How far that little candle throws his beams!
> So shines a good deed in a naughty world!"

Then you fall to making a series of quaint, but wholesome similes, and you begin by considering that after all, if you *are* a hypochondriac, and have conceived yourself to be even that most disgraceful of cereous concoctions, a Confederate candle, there is some analogy and truth in the illusion; for, is it not thus our fleeting life melts away in this rude world?—and if **you are righteous** adamantine, and not impure tallow, will **you not burn** the brighter, and shine **the** farther for it?—**if the rude winds of** sorrow assail you, will you not flicker, and gutter, **and melt** away the sooner?—if you do not trim your wick, now and then **with a** pair of moral snuffers, will you not run, and drip, and splutter, and become an abomination in the eyes of all good people?—and **are** there not moments in your weary captivity, oh, *wicked* prisoner! when you wish some merciful gush of the winter wind through the iron bars would *blow you out*, and be done with it!

The sentinel under my window is crying out at the **top of his voice:** "Nine o'clock! lights out!"

As I creep in between my blankets I feel that I owe something **to that poor candle** for the little sermon it has preached **to me. I shall** wander off now into the empyrean fields of a pre-slumberous reverie— a sort of nocturnal **campaign against** the evils of discontent, with my dollar's worth of morality in my haversack—and ere I fall asleep I shall be sure to have strayed on, and on, very far into the future, or perhaps even to the doors of that eternal prison, narrower, and colder, and darker, than the Libby, at whose threshold Death, the grim sentinel, will cry out, "Nine o'clock! lights out!" and I will answer as I have done to-night:

"Out, out, brief candle!"

People are in the habit of speaking of the *other* world, as if there were but two: I would suggest that there are three—the third is the *Prison World*.

In the species of posthumous existence which the prisoner leads, the memories of the past, the kindly sympathies, expressed in tender messages, of the dear ones far away in the sphere of a real life, the affectionate tokens which reach him warm from the hearts of unforgetting friends—all these seem but like the echoes of familiar voices borne to him from another world.

The life of the prison-house is simply inhuman, unnatural. Different minds are no doubt affected to a different degree by it; but whatever the mental constitution, it must be influenced to a certain extent, and deflected, as it were, from its habitual angle. The speculative become morbid and misanthropic; the excitable and buoyant, languishing from the lack of mental stimulus, sink by reaction into the stagnation of a morbid apathy. It is the calm and philosophical who are best calculated to endure the weary monotony and the tedious routine of prison life. Not but that most men are apt to become to some extent selfish and irascible under suffering and privation; but the one naturally callous and uncharitable becomes repulsively egotistical, and the one naturally ill-tempered converts himself into an insupportable monster, actuated by the ferocity of the bear, and bristling all over with the quills of the porcupine. But if the bad qualities of some are so forcibly developed, the good in others are apt to expand in the same ratio: the amiable become almost feminine in their kindness; the generous carry their liberality into improvidence; the charitable become self-sacrificing in their bounty; —to such, the influences of prison life are fraught with beneficial tendencies. Religion, the child of woe, cradled in humility, and reared in misfortune, takes a deeper root in their hearts. The mind lacking occupation turns inevitably to thought,—thought leads it to investigation—investigation to truth. The daily contemplation of suffering and misery, of helplessness and want, teach the necessity of faith—and faith is the leaf of that plant whose blossoms are of hope. Cut off from comforts and tender sympathies

—from the daily intercourse of friends—from the habitual avocations of life—shut out **from** social pleasures—doomed to the tedium of a solitude which is the heaviest **to bear**: **the solitude of the heart**; **and to a melancholy** which **is the saddest**: **in which day after day, and month after month, the same gloomy scenes are contemplated, the same cold faces beheld, the same narrow circle walked,—he is lost indeed, who loses hope.**

Imprisonment **generally renders men serious—with that seriousness of the heart which lifts it to purer thoughts, and to better actions.** No place, surely, is better adapted **than the prison-house for the study of human nature. Suffering develops the real character.** It is in the midst of bodily or mental anguish that we are apt to cast off the **mask** unreservedly, and indeed, unawares. **This is a** crucible **to the heart.** In such an imprisonment as **ours, there is no privacy;** there are no moments of truce for **hypocrisy—of** rest for the daily wearing of the mask; we live continually as if in the midst of a crowded street—held up to the observation of the curious—always under the eye of some one. Under such circumstances, that goodness must indeed be sterling which never forgets itself, and that merit genuine which stands firmly upon its pedestal to the last.

Captivity is a flail which threshes the chaff out of human pride. Men are not apt to be supercilious when they are starving; they suffer, and must bow; they are tortured, and must yield. They must battle against idleness, and they become diligent; they must elude their implacable foe, ennui, every hour of the day and every day of the month, and when their resources are exhausted they must stoop to trivial pursuits and pastimes to baffle their enemy,—being no longer able to amuse themselves as men, they remember how they used to amuse themselves when they were children. They are surprised to find that the whittling of toy-boats and playing at jack-straws, and romping like school-boys, can afford even a passing occupation.

All silly pride and squeamishness must be set aside: the future brigadier must sit, barefoot, with a bucket between his legs, while he washes his own stockings; the dashing cavalry officer, who led that glorious charge of which the newspapers were so full, must inevitably serve his turn at cooking and scouring, like a good patriotic cook and scullion that he is,— he must accommodate his genius to circumstances, and display as much gallantry in charging a row of cook-pots as he did in scattering a battalion of the enemy's cavalry.

It is curious to see with what earnestness and alacrity every branch of learning is undertaken. There have been at different times in the prison, classes of French, German, Spanish, Italian, Latin and Greek, English Grammar, Phonography, Fencing, Dancing, Military Tactics and a Bible Class. Of course this educational enthusiasm is very ephemeral; these studies are taken up with avidity, to be dropped in disgust at an early day. What the prisoner seeks, in most cases, is not so much instruction as novelty —not so much information as amusement;—much good is no doubt derived from this morbid thirst, for here and there a good seed takes root in a fruitful brain, and glimpses are afforded into the rich arcana of science which may, at some future period, lead to more substantial results. The prison-world must have its educational system; the student turns down the leaf of his Natural Philosophy to set to work at chopping his hash; he lays down his Logic or his Rhetoric to go to the trough to wash his shirt. This is a capital system—for it renders the student humble, while it makes him learned—and this humility will in after life, rather add to than detract from the merit of his wisdom. He is compelled to learn something of housekeeping also—which will prove of great benefit to him in matrimony, and which will be considered by his wife decidedly charming and **economical.** Indeed, no system of training could be better adapted to prepare a young man for the duties, the responsibilities, the vicissitudes, and may I with all deference be permitted to add, the little counter-revolutions of married life.

He learns something of the real world too: he studies it by contrast; he learns properly to appreciate the evils of idleness, the blessings of freedom, the sympathy of friends, the necessity of social communion; he learns, by sad experience, how many blessings there are in the world, which he had ignored. **If gratitude be indeed** the memory **of the** heart, he **feels how bright that memory should be** ever kept **by those who have never** read **their own** names written **in the** book of suffering, as well as by those **who have thumbed its** dreary pages **in the prison-house.**

Most people's notions about imprisonment are con**nected with the idea of** an unbroken solitude; of **that** constant association with self, which no heart, however gifted and pure, and **no** mind, however fruitful in resources and **rich in** lore, can long withstand without drooping into weariness, and languishing into melancholy. With **us,** here, the **case is** in many respects different. More than a thousand human beings crowded into the narrow limits of the prison, subjected to the same trials and privations, forced constantly into one another's society, and continually under each other's eyes, we suffer intensely from the want of that very privacy of which the victim of solitary confinement has too much.

This forcing together of spirits often uncongenial, of diverse tastes, and antagonistical ideas, is a curse to the mind.

This jamming together of hapless mortality, this endless "crush of matter," and ceaseless shock of tortured humanity, is a curse to the body.

The prison is crowded to its utmost capacity; every nook and corner is occupied; we jostle each other at the hydrants, on the stairs, around the cooking stoves; at night we must calculate closely the horizontal space required on the floor for the proper distribution of our recumbent anatomy. Everywhere there is crowding, wrangling and confusion.

"If there is society where none intrudes," there is surely very little of it where the intruders are so numerous. As to being exclusive—the attempt would be preposterous;—as to living secluded—that is out of the question. You are in a whirlpool, and you must keep whirling round daily with the merciless eddy in a sort of diabolical gyration. This is apt to render one irascible and crabbed, and sometimes even unjust,—which horribly jangles that precious little silver bell in the human heart—*good nature*, wont at times to ring out, amid the wilder chimes, such pleasant music!

To add to the unwholesomeness, and to the inconveniences of such a mode of life, we are allowed no out-door exercise. The prison is too much crowded to admit of our walking about with any degree of comfort. Some of the prisoners now here, have not once stepped outside the prison door during more than eight months!

Perhaps no periods of our prison life are so trying as those melancholy episodes in it connected with our cooking experiences.

I feel constrained to devote a few remarks to this subject, in view of the probable benefits to be derived from them, in future times, by such unfortunate military gentlemen as may be condemned to pass through the smoky ordeal of a prison cook-house; for, a soldier, however much accustomed to stand fire, will occasionally find himself, under such circumstances, in a place quite as hot as the battle-field, and unless he pay some attention to the theory and practice of

14*

minor strategy, he will more than once be compelled to go dinnerless.

You are reminded by the members of your mess, (whose memories seldom prove treacherous in this connection,) that it is your turn to cook. If you are in a large mess your tour of duty will be of two or three days' duration; if you are in a small one, it will last, perhaps, a week.

The first question you ask of yourself, when this gratifying information is conveyed to you, is apt to be this: "What shall we have for dinner?" The same question is being asked every day, and has been, since time immemorial, by ingenious housewives with reduced larders; you have probably heard it yourself more than once at home, perchance during the happy years of your improvident adolescence, and you may now philosophize a little upon the supreme inconvenience, under peculiar circumstances, of having to answer this question.

In the Libby, to be sure, you will not be quite so much puzzled for a reply. "Let me see," you will soliloquize, casting an anxious and searching glance at your boxes and shelves, "we have corn-bread, and vinegar, and salt, and pepper, and a little rye-coffee, and . . ." Here you will pause and scratch your head, for it is very awkward to finish a sentence with a conjunction; but you will have **to waive your** grammatical scruples, **and resign yourself to the commission** of a harmless **solecism**; for you will probably recollect that there is an unprofitable "and" at the end of every thing, pretty much, about the Libby, where "ands" are as common as are "ifs" in the outer world, and unfortunately quite as useless. So, finding that your "and" must remain in hopeless celibacy owing to the absence of any edible to wed it to, you will take up your **corn-bread and study what you** may concoct out of it, or how **you may disguise it, and make it look like something else than so** much baked saw-dust; **you may grate it down**—(Oh, shade of Soyer!) saturate it with water, **and fashion it into the semblance of a corn-meal pudding**; **or, you** may fry it, with pork-fat, into corn-cakes—or, . . . **but** your "or" may prove quite as troublesome to **you as** your "and,"—so you decide upon the *pudding*, which **sounds so** homelike and civilized. You mix your pudding, and with it on a tin plate in one hand, and your coffee-pot in the other, you proceed down to the cook-room.

You find the cook-room crowded **to** suffocation, the latter process being admirably facilitated by the cloud of impenetrable smoke which is the prevailing atmosphere of the cook-world; the stoves are completely covered with all sorts of ingenious culinary contrivances in the shape of pots, skillets, pans, mugs, and cans, and to back this formidable assortment of motley utensils, is an army of ferocious cooks, armed with ladles, forks, and spoons, all struggling to look into their "stews" at one and the same time—an operation which is utterly impracticable where only three small stoves are to render edible so large a quantity of the most uncookable and indigestible materials.

You marvel why it is that all these insane men should have been seized with the unreasonable whim of cooking just at that particular time, when the members of *your* mess expect you to prepare *their* dinner. You wait a long time, standing there, and staring vacantly, and painfully too, through the thick smoke; the aspect of affairs is very unpromising, but you must arrive at some decision: your messmates will not agree with you that it would be more wholesome to dine after dark; so, you advance a few steps, and make a frantic effort to wedge yourself in between those fratricidal cooks. In all probability some crabbed fellow lets fall upon your legs a little summer shower of scalding water; or, some piratical looking foreigner, with overgrown moustaches curled up at the ends like a pair of infuriated scorpions, runs the handle of a ponderous ladle into your ribs; or, an accidental back-hander from some gigantic Hoosier jostles a fair proportion of your ground coffee into your eyes;—but you must push on bravely, regardless of all personal peril, and persevere undismayed until you have had your toes trodden upon for the hundredth time—until you are red in the face as a dry-weather moon—until you have smutted your nose, and burnt your fingers—until you are half stifled, half distracted, and completely disgusted—until, in fine, you have baked your pudding, and rescued the voracious members of your mess from presenting a melancholy instance of Confederate starvation.

Then the dinner—that is to say, the pudding—over, you must remove your coat and roll up your sleeves, and go to work at "washing up the things." You make a great ado with your soft soap and hot water, looking for all the world, as you loom up out of a cloud of greasy steam, like a species of domestic cherub; and you rub, and splash, and scour—presenting a picture which would stir to the very core the good old heart of your maternal grandmother!

Then, too, you must be very careful that the "things" are safe. You must keep an eye to them until they pass into the keeping of your successor; for pilfering is not deemed a cardinal sin in the

Libby; your tin dippers and your pewter spoons are apt to be spirited away in the most miraculous manner, and your little store of eatables diminishes, at times, most unaccountably. Borrowing is safe to practice; but lending is an imprudence against which you must guard, unless you are thoroughly convinced of the integrity and previous good character of the borrower. We were lately compelled to carve upon the coffee-pot of our mess, the following significant inscription:

"To borrow, is human—to return, divine."

An order from Major Turner was read to us a few days since, to the effect that henceforth we will be permitted to write home but one letter per week—no letter to exceed *six lines*. This is a severe limitation. The only unalloyed pleasure we experience in our imprisonment is the writing and receiving of letters. Much ingenuity must be exercised to enable one to crowd into six lines the thousand messages expected at our hands by mothers, wives, and sweethearts. The following is a model specimen from an incarcerated husband to his afflicted spouse:

"My Dear Wife:

"Yours received—no hope of exchange—send cornstarch—want socks—no money—rheumatism in the left shoulder—pickles very good—send sausages—God bless you—kiss the baby,—Hail Columbia!

"Your devoted
"HUSBAND."

The 8th of this month has been one of the most eventful in the history of our prison-life. It will be long remembered on account of the escape of more than a hundred of our number from bondage; some, destined to reach the Federal lines in safety; others, less fortunate, doomed to be recaptured, and to suffer additional tortures at the hands of our keepers.

As far back as last fall, various attempts had been made by officers confined in the prison, under the direction of Colonel Rose of the 77th Pennsylvania, to excavate a tunnel, through which they might hope to effect their escape. To Colonel Rose is chiefly due the credit of these explorations. Animated by an unflinching earnestness of purpose, unwearying perseverance, and no ordinary engineering abilities, he organized, at different times, working parties of ten or fifteen officers, whom he conducted every night into the cellars of the prison. These cellars were very dark, and entirely unguarded, being seldom visited, even in the day time. To these they descended through an opening in the flooring of the room above them used as a kitchen for the prisoners; this opening was carefully concealed by a well-fitted board during the day.

The earliest excavation made led directly into a stratum of rock, and was soon abandoned as impracticable. The next attempt was made in the direction of the main sewer, which runs under the street between the prison and the canal. The plan was to dig from the cellar into this sewer, and by creeping through it, to gain the street at a safe distance from the prison, by means of one of the inlets. After many nights of labor, performed under the most trying circumstances, water began to filter into the excavation, and finally poured in so rapidly that it was impossible to continue the work. This tunnel was abandoned with the greatest reluctance; it was admirably planned, and had it proved successful, would no doubt have emptied the prison of its inmates in a few hours. Several thrilling incidents occurred in connection with it. The cellar from which it was started was sometimes used as a workshop, and a carpenter's table stood directly under the aperture through which the nocturnal diggers dropped down nightly from the kitchen above. The descent and ascent were made by means of a rope

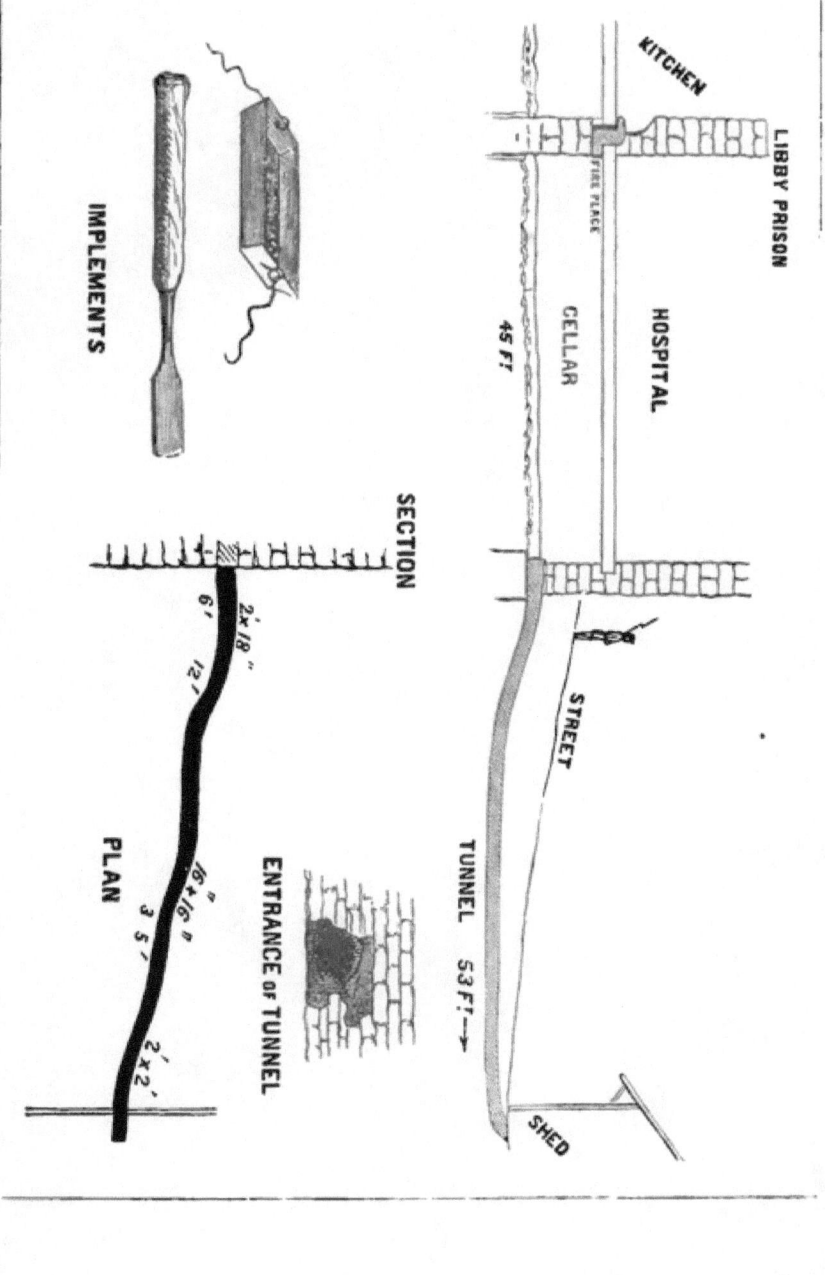

or blanket. One night, as one of the officers was being drawn up, the rope broke and he fell from a height of several feet upon the table. His fall made a fearful racket. A sentry whose beat was within a few yards of the locality of this untoward accident, immediately called out for the corporal of the guard. After a lengthy and profound discussion as to what might have occasioned this unusual noise, both the corporal and the sentry ascribed it to some trifling cause, and no further notice was taken of it.

Another night Colonel Rose was digging under the very beat of a sentinel, when a small portion of the earth and pavement caved in. The sentinel, attracted by the circumstance, ran immediately to the spot. "What is it?" asked the soldier at the next post. "A thundering big rat," cried the first one, running his bayonet into the hole. The point of the bayonet grazed the Colonel's cheek. He remained for a long time motionless and almost breathless, until the unsuspecting sentinel resumed his beat, little dreaming what were the real proportions of this Federal *rat!*

After many fruitless attempts to penetrate into the sewers, it was resolved to make an effort to tunnel under the street east of the prison, and to reach the yard of a ware-house opposite. This street was paced day and night by sentinels. Early in January, Colonel Rose organized a working party of fourteen officers, who were to relieve each other regularly in the work, one always remaining on guard near the excavation to prevent a trap being set for the capture of the remainder of the party, in case of discovery by the prison officials. Having succeeded in lifting out the bottom of the fire-place in the cook-room, they removed the bricks from the back of the flue, and penetrated between the floor joists into the cellar, under the end room used as a hospital. Passing through this aperture, they could with facility lower each other down into the cellar. An opening was commenced in the wall near the northeast corner of the cellar. This opening was about two feet by eighteen inches. It was found necessary to cut through the piles on which the building was supported, and this tedious labor was at length successfully completed with no other tools but pocket knives. As they penetrated into the earth, great difficulty was experienced on account of the candles, which refused to burn in the close air of the tunnel. One of the party was compelled to stand constantly at the opening, fanning air into it with his hat. The tunnel fell with a slight depression for a distance of about twelve feet, then continued slightly ascending for about the same distance, and was nearly level the remainder of its length. It was about fifty-three feet long. The first depression was rendered necessary by the fall of the ground towards the ware-house.

The tunnel, at its entrance, was about two feet by eighteen inches, and for some six feet of its length ran at right angles with the street, it then turned a few degrees to the right with a diameter of only sixteen inches, and continued at this angle increasing gradually to a diameter of about two feet to its exit. In order to pass through, it was necessary, of course, to lie flat on one's face, propelling oneself with the hands and feet, as the space was not sufficient to allow of creeping on hands and knees.

As they approached the yard of the warehouse, a slight error in the computation of the distance nearly proved fatal to the enterprise. Thinking they had reached the enclosure, they dug up to the surface and upon breaking through discovered that they had come out in the street, outside the fence, and within a few yards of the sentinels. This hole was quickly filled up with a pair of old pants and some straw, and the digging was continued a few feet further to the desired point under a shed in the yard. An empty hogshead was drawn over the opening to conceal it in the daytime. During more than three weeks this severe labor had been perseveringly carried on. The only implements used were a large chisel furnished with a long handle, and a wooden spit-box brought down from one of the rooms above; to each end of this box a cord was attached, by which it could be drawn into the tunnel and filled with the removed earth by the digger, and drawn out by his assistant. The earth and gravel thus taken out was carefully concealed under some straw and rubbish in the cellar.

On the night of the 8th, the tunnel was finally pronounced practicable for the proposed escape of the party. About twenty-five of the prisoners are said to have been in the secret; these were to make their escape early in the evening, and were to have two hours start; after that, the rest of the prisoners were to be informed, and all who were strong enough to make the attempt were to be allowed to go out.

Colonel Streight and his party were the first to go, and succeeded in making their way out undetected. Once in the yard of the warehouse, they had but to pass out through a gate into the street, between the two lines of guards, and walk boldly away along the canal. During the night one hundred and nine of the officers thus made their escape. Of these only fifty-three have succeeded in reaching the Federal lines. The remainder have been recaptured at different points along the roads leading down to the Peninsula, and are now in the dungeons under the prison, on corn-bread and water. Colonel Rose, to whose protracted labors and untiring zeal, the final success of the plan of escape was mainly due, is unfortunately among the recaptured. After a series of thrilling adventures and narrow escapes, he had succeeded in approaching within a mile or two of Williamsburg, where he deemed himself safe from further pursuit. While resting by the roadside, he was approached by two soldiers dressed in the Federal uniform; convinced that they were Union soldiers, he did not hesitate, in answer to their questions, to state who he was. They proved to be Rebel scouts. After they had taken him at a full run more than a mile out of the way of the Federal scouts and pickets who were close by, one of the Rebels left. Colonel Rose, though well nigh overcome with exhaustion, and fainting from hunger, made one last desperate effort for his liberty. Springing suddenly upon the remaining Rebel, he clutched him by the throat, and endeavored to throw him to the ground and disarm him; he was so feeble, however, that after a brief struggle his strength entirely deserted him. He had contrived to get his finger on the trigger of his opponent's musket, and had discharged the piece during the struggle. The report of the gun having brought back the other scout, Colonel Rose was then secured and brought once more into the Confederate lines.

We are now subjected, in the prison, to an endless ordeal of roll calls, and every precaution is being taken by Major Turner to prevent any further attempts at escape. This rigid exercise of vigilance comes, of course, a day too late, and will not make up for the late laxity of discipline about the prison. Indeed it is wonderful how the grand escapade could have been effected without detection. During the exodus, at about midnight, a sudden panic seized the crowd of prisoners who were gathered about the fireplace in the cook-room, all endeavoring to be the first to get out through the tunnel. Some one said the guard was coming, and a general stampede took place up the stairways to the rooms above, with a frightful noise of feet, and oversetting of boxes and barrels, that must have been heard a square off. But the guards did not suspect what was in progress; one of them, indeed, was heard to call out jocosely to a companion on the next beat "Halloa, Bill—there's somebody's coffee-pot upset, sure!"

The recaptured officers give many thrilling accounts of their adventures. One party got into a boat on the James River, and followed the stream in the hope of reaching Hampton Roads. Unfortunately they got into the Appomattox River by mistake, where their little craft was upset in the darkness of the night, and they were compelled to take to the shore, nearly frozen to death. The next morning they were discovered by some Rebel soldiers and recaptured. Another party had concealed themselves in the swamps near the Chickahominy, where they were hunted out by the aid of dogs and finally secured.

Among the escaped are the following Field Officers:

Colonel A. D. Streight, 51st Indiana.
" Thomas E. Rose, 77th Pennsylvania.*
" C. W. Tilden, 16th Maine.
" W. G. Ely, 18th Connecticut.*
" W. B. McCreary, 16th Maine.
" W. P. Kendrick, N. Tennessee Cavalry.
Lieutenant-Colonel J. C. Boyd, Quartermaster's Department.
" " D. E. Miles, 79th Pennsylvania.*
" " J. C. Spofford, 97th New York.*
" " J. Walker, 5th Kentucky Cavalry.
" " E. L. Hayes, 100th Ohio.*
" " C. H. Morton, Kentucky Cavalry.
" " T. G. West, 24th Wisconsin.

Lieutenant-Colonel H. C. Hobart, 21st Wisconsin.
Major J. H. Hooper, 15th Massachusetts.
" Mulholland, 30th Indiana.
" Von Mitzell, 74th Pennsylvania.
" Fitzsimmons, 30th Indiana.
" B. B. McDonald, 101st Ohio.
" J. P. Collins, 29th Indiana.
" J. Henry, 6th Ohio Cavalry.*

Those marked with a star were retaken.

Of the Line Officers thirty were Captains, and fifty-eight were Lieutenants.

The recaptured officers state that they were treated with kindness by those who retook them,—especially by the officers and soldiers on duty in the neighborhood of the Chickahominy. Indeed, it was not until their return to the prison, where they were locked up in the cells on bread and water, that they experienced any harsh or unsoldierlike treatment.

THE DUNGEON.

"Paroled," a prison dream.

IX.

1864.

March:—Reveries—Matter of Fact—Matrimonial—Consolatory—Rumors—Huckster Officers—Confederate Currency and Prices—"Tunnel on the Brain"—A Search—Boxes—General Kilpatrick's Raid—The Gunpowder Plot—Paroled—Conclusion.

REVERIES.

REVERY is the presentiment of the heart: the visions it evokes are but our hopes made visible.

The prisoner has ample time, and an ample field for thought. He *must* think; and he cannot think without dreaming.

He sees the hour arrive when the prison doors are thrown open; he drinks in eagerly the first breaths of the pure, untainted air; he sees the blue sky, nothing but the deep gulf of the sky, above him—an eternity of space; the sun dazzles him with the radiant splendor of its light, and its rays fall, warm and genial upon him, like a glorious rain of golden fire. He feels himself borne with a speed all too slow for his love, swiftly, swiftly, over the water, and over the echoing rails; he stands at the threshold of his home, breathless, panting, the heart almost pulseless with happiness; his mother's, **sister's**, wife's, children's arms are about his neck; there is a volcano of hearty greetings—a whirlwind of happy words—a hurricane of kisses! The dream has culminated, but the dreamer does not relax his mind's hold upon it; he clings to it with a sort of child-like tenacity, until the brain can retain it no longer, and the bright vision fades—a purple flame—farther and farther, to wane at last like a fainting star, in the cold daylight of reality!

If the asperities of an active campaign are calculated to moderate the romantic ardor with which the incipient soldier looks forward to the glorious experiences of the camp and the battle-field, a six months' incarceration in a Richmond prison may not unreasonably be expected to dissipate the last lingering vestige, which may still float vapor-like through his brain, of what is in any way connected with the romantic and the sentimental.

We are not Lion-hearted Richards here, who list at the turret casement of a new Tenebreuse, for the harp and the song of a faithful Blondel; we are not Byronical Bonnivards chained in the dungeons of a modern Chillon, and destined to leave our prison "with a sigh;" this is no Spielburg to be rendered classical by a thousand Silvio Pellicos;—it is only a plain matter of fact warehouse, dating back only a dozen years into the past,—a rectangular, unturreted, unbattlemented brick house, with a James River for its Danube—a canal for its lake Leman—and the rear of a row of brick dwellings for its Moravian hills.

Very little of the romantic there is about a captivity in which the cutting up of a hash, the washing of a pair of socks, and the scouring of a cook-pot, are among the unavoidable contingencies of daily life. There is nothing of the heroic about it. The prisoner may urge a claim to sympathy, not for what he does, but rather for what he cannot do,—for what he suffers, and not for what he achieves. His is a negative and abnormal condition: a soldier without a sword—a man with all the helplessness of a child,— if he is not fed, he must starve—if he is not clothed he must go naked,—he is a gentleman who cooks his own dinner, does his own washing, manufactures his own furniture, mends his own clothes, and cobbles his own shoes; he may be rich enough at home, but here he must rest contented with the meagre pittance of pin-money which may doled out to him from time to time; he is, in fine, the most deplorable human being that can be conceived of. But few in the world are so wretched, and so poor, that they cannot creep out where the fresh wind blows, and the sun shines, and feel that the wholesome air and the warm glow of Heaven, are blessings as boundless for him as for the richest! What poverty is equal to the isolation from the exciting avocations of the field, the comforts of home,—to the prison penury of air and light—the misery of idleness—the famine for action—the thirst for liberty?

Of all poetry the most unsubstantial is the poetry of sorrow—it is the poetry of the plant which withers that its fruit may ripen. Bonnivard would no doubt have been much better satisfied with his long captivity in the castle of Chillon, had he been able to while away the tedium of his prison hours by reading Byron's superb manner of immortalizing his imprisonment.

But there are some forms of suffering and sorrow which baffle the most skilful alchemy of the poet; for it is seldom that he can stoop gracefully from the spiritual to the purely material. Let him paint if he can, the poetry of hunger, at a breakfast made up of a tin plate, a pewter spoon, and a very small onion; of a hard blanket-bed on a bare floor; let him, if he can, extract passion from the tasteless solidity of cold corn bread,—evaporate romance out of the vapid impurities of James River water,—resolve into ideality the rancid impracticabilities of Confederate bacon,— or worry sentiment out of the greasy convolutions of a Richmond sausage!

It is a fact, I dare say not generally ignored, that many of the natives of Bulgaria are in the habit of emigrating to Constantinople, where they either become traders, or, what is more usual, earn an honest livelihood by all sorts of manual labor. These are mostly newly married men, who, after a number of years of separation from their young wives,—years spent in amassing their little fortune,—return home richer by their savings, to spend the remainder of their lives, contentedly and happily, in their comfortable homes.

I do not know exactly how this fact about the sensible bridegrooms of Bulgaria happened to creep into my inkstand; but I suspect it was owing to the alarming rumors, just now prevalent, of the permanent suspension of the cartel for the exchange of prisoners, and the strong probability of our being compelled to remain in captivity during the entire continuance of the war. It has occurred to me that it would be as well for us to settle down in Libby in good earnest,—to send home for furniture and all the appurtenances of civilized domesticity,—marry some patriotic Northern girl by proxy,—and make ourselves as comfortable and cosey as possible. Then, the war over, we may with good grace plunge all at once, *à la Bulgarian*, into the consummate blissfulness of a home, and feel that our years of captivity have not been a mere useless void.

The monotonous routine of prison life is not the most grievous of its evils. We are surprised, on looking back upon the past days of our prison history, to feel that weeks and months seem to have slipped away so quickly:—this surprise is wholesome. Memory, in reviewing the past, depends upon marked incidents to guide it: "on such a day I was captured;" "In such a year I entered the army," are the kind of remarks with which the mind is apt to assist memory. By such aid it computes the relative dates of the occurrence of events,—these events are its landmarks. The more of these landmarks memory can see, the more it remembers of past life. Over the monotonous uniformity of prison life, memory wanders back as over a trackless shore, and its landmarks are so few, that it sweeps over the breadth of months with a swiftness, by which, to be deceived is to be benefited. Were it not for this melting away of trivial incidents into an oblivious vacuity, what mind, however strongly fortified behind the ramparts of philosophy, could bear the fearful burthen of all the tedium of the present multiplied by all the tedium of the past? This waveless sea over which time sails on, and leaves no wake,—this Sahara over which the little caravan of daily sorrows journeys on its way to Lethe, and on which the foot-marks of to-day are buried under the shifted sands of to-morrow,—such as it is, is better than too clear a record of an episode in our lives which could not be too vividly remembered without a shudder, nor all unveiled without a sigh.

"Enter Rumor—painted all over with tongues," might head a chapter of Libby life with quite as much pertinence as the opening scene in a Shakespearean tragedy.

These rumors are generally about the exchange of prisoners, or Rebel retaliation; but when these prolific subjects have been temporarily exhausted, new tongues are painted on the imp's motley garb. The fact is, that I suspect Rumor to be the child of Idleness; for it is those among the prisoners who are seldom seen to read, study, or devote their time to any rational occupation, who premeditate and circulate such startling reports as "an immediate exchange of prisoners"—"flag of truce boat just up," or "lots to be drawn for hanging."

It is no wonder that I am called aside some twenty times a day by some lugubrious hypochondriac, and mysteriously informed that "Oh, it is horrible! too horrible to think of!—The Rebels have raised the black flag, and ten Federal officers are to be hung, every day for the next three weeks, in retaliation for an equal number slaughtered in cold blood by Butler!" (probably for his breakfast.) Or perhaps it is some youthful and excitable Second Lieutenant on the highway to promotion by the War Department, and to lionization by a score of patriotic young ladies at the North, who taps me on the shoulder, accompanying this jocose and amiable manifestation by an expressive wink of his favorite eye, and who whispers in my ear (loud enough to be heard all over the room) that "the commissioners have met, and have agreed to a general exchange, and that in less than a week we will all be out!" And away he goes, smacking his lips over the savor of a premature brandy-punch at Willard's, or a dim-visioned goblet of Heidsick at "an evening party at home."

It requires all the philosophy and stoicism acquired by a long acquaintance with this sort of prison necromancy, and the vivid recollection of numberless very bitter disappointments, to enable one to arrive at the conclusion that the "hanging" and the "punch" are the one about as likely to transpire as the other—with some degree of probability, and certainly the "advantage of position," in favor of the former.

Among the many curious and interesting operations of the human mind, none appeal to us more forcibly than those which are the result of habit, or are due to the influences of education. The merchant continues to invest, long after the acquisition of affluence has lifted him above the necessity of speculation; the actor, long retired from the stage, still walks the highway of real life with something of his professional strut; the sailor, in his old age, still fixes a shrewd glance upon the gathering cloud, and watches the changing wind; the old soldier, propped by his crutch, beholds in the world but another battle-field, lives strategically, and dies with the word of command on his lips.

I am led to these reflections by a sight which I repeatedly witness here, in the prison: that of Federal officers, in full uniform, sitting behind barrels, and peddling apples and segars to their fellow-prisoners. These enterprising, if unsoldierly

—and ingenious, if undignified, gentlemen—must present a broad and interesting field for philosophical investigation **to the Confederate strangers who** visit our prison. For, what though it be no crime against humanity to peddle apples at five for a dollar, or segars at thirty-seven and a half cents a piece, in a Rebel prison, **it might have** occurred to these huckster-gentlemen, that neither the **brick** walls nor iron **bars of** the Libby can, with good grace, transmute a commissioned officer in the service of the United States, into a segar pedlar, **or an** apple dealer. There is but one conclusion which can explain this anomaly, and it is a profoundly philosophical one : these gentlemen are the creatures of habit.

The steady and significant depreciation of the Confederate currency may be judged of by the fact that in July, 1863, a one dollar United States Treasury note was valued at four dollars in Confederate scrip ; in August at six ; in September and October, at seven ; in November, at ten ; in December, at twelve ; in January, 1864, as high as twenty. A gentleman's coat will cost about $300 ; a lady's bonnet $250 ; a pair of shoes $50 ; a pair of chickens $20 ; a pound of sugar $5 ; a small loaf of wheat bread $1; a box of matches 25 cents. The monthly pay of a Rebel soldier is eleven dollars!

The great escapade through **the** tunnel seems to have completely destroyed the mental equilibrium of our young Commandant of the Prison, Major Turner. He seems determined that not another prisoner shall escape from his clutches, and spares no precaution to insure our safe-keeping. The iron bars in the windows have been strengthened, and rendered impregnable. A corporal's guard patrols the building every two hours during the night, (to the tune of the "Rogue's March," whistled by the unterrified captives as they lie in their blankets); this patrol examines carefully every fire-place, window, nook, and corner, of every room. Major Turner seems to have been suddenly seized with the frantic idea that we **might tunnel** ourselves out of a third-story window, **or that we might** be constructing a huge balloon **wherewith to elevate** ourselves from the roof of the **prison!**

We have now roll-calls without number. We are counted and recounted, from morning until night. Even in the middle of the night we have been waked up out of our blankets to be counted, because one of the sentries happening to look down into a sewer at the corner of the street, imagined that he saw a "Yankee," or the shadow of one, crawling up out of the inlet—when, no doubt, it was his own shadow that he saw.

Any one late at roll-call is compelled to stand up under guard, in the kitchen, for four hours. Yesterday I saw a row of five or six thus standing against the wall, for being late.

A day or two ago we were all ordered down into the kitchen, a room one hundred feet by forty-five. We were, one thousand in number, crowded into that filthy apartment. The smoke was so thick that it was with difficulty we could breathe. Even *Dick* Turner, the Warden (whose cruelty has, evidently, been much exaggerated) was softened at the sight; he went to Major Turner, and begged that we might be allowed to occupy one of the rooms up stairs. But the fossilized little Commandant was inflexible:

"You have heard my orders, Sir," said he, no doubt raising high his belligerent eye-brows, striking his spurred heels together with a very warlike and most imposing jingle, and dismissing poor Dick with a senatorial wave of his right hand, "you have heard my orders, Sir, and they—must—be—obeyed!"

"But," persisted the lesser Turner, "they will be choked to death with the smoke, and——"

"Hem!" interrupted the pompous little Commandant, curling his hairless lip which looked as though a moustache was *afraid* to grow there, and coughing a portentous cough which sounded as though he had another pair of spurs in his throat.

Poor Dick felt that in such a cough might indeed be involved the future destinies of the whole Confederacy,—so back he came to us, and in that suffocating kitchen we had to stand, jammed together, during four mortal hours.

What was going on up stairs?

What was all this about?

It was a search for miners' tools, and fire-arms!

I would not wonder if our bewildered little Commandant really suspected that he might discover among our poor empty boxes, and our dilapidated wardrobes, at the very least a battery of Parrot guns, a train of ammunition wagons, a derrick or two, muskets and pistols, picks, spades, shovels, saws, hammers, and who knows what not!

When we returned to our quarters, we found all our little files and tools, used for bone cutting (and some of the bone-work too)—gone! All villainous-looking pocket-knives—gone! Whatever had an edge, or a tooth, or a point—gone! Whatever looked as though it might be useful in lifting out the bottom of a fireplace, or digging a hole—gone!

Really,—when our distracted little Commandant now comes into our rooms, he keeps his knees well together,—it is necessary to be very cautious,—some of us might slip out between his legs!

Our boxes from home, or rather a portion of their contents, are being again delivered to us. We are no longer permitted to be present when they are opened. Captain Monroe, who has now charge of the delivery of boxes to us, has, I dare say, made this new arrangement, in order to spare our feelings in cases of confiscation. The boxes are now opened in a warehouse on the opposite side of the street, and such proportion of their contents as is deemed consistent with Captain Monroe's ideas of honesty and fair dealing between enemies, is doled out to us in blankets which we carry down to the street-door for that purpose. Yesterday one officer received as *his* share of his own box, two Northern newspapers and a Bologna sausage; another one was rendered happy and comfortable by being given, out of the contents of a barrel, a package of salt and three tin candlesticks!

During the recent three months of starvation, we

could see our boxes piled up in the warehouses near the prison, whilst we had hard work to keep soul and body together upon prison rations; and every night we could hear these boxes being broken open and pillaged. All this was in retaliation, we heard, for the alleged stoppage of boxes sent from here to Rebel prisoners at the North. But why refuse to give us even the coffee and sugar sent us by our families, when coffee and sugar are regular rations given to Rebel prisoners in the Northern prisons?

Why confiscate, wholesale, the boxes sent by Sanitary and other charitable Societies at the North?

Oh, what a lucky hitch for the Rebels in the box question!

Some days ago we sent money, through the Warden, to purchase some under clothing in Richmond. Upon receiving the articles sent for, we were not a little surprised to discover stamped on them in blue letters: "Sanitary Commission. Philadelphia." Upon reproaching Mr. Dick Turner for this rather unfair proceeding of selling us articles which it was intended should be distributed to us gratuitously, he replied with such charming impudence that we could not get angry with him, "Why, gentlemen—they are a d——d sight better goods than you could buy any where in Richmond, for the same money!"

When it became known, a few days ago, that General Kilpatrick had crossed the Rappahannock and was on his way to Richmond, with the probable design of liberating the Union prisoners confined here, the excitement was tremendous. We had suspected that something unusual was occurring from the fact that we could not obtain the daily papers, and from the hurried movement of troops over the bridges across the James river, and through the streets, within sight of the prison. All the city troops and home guards were sent to the front. Indeed, among the killed and wounded in the engagement at Green's Farm, were some of the very soldiers who had stood guard, a few days before, around our prison.

The stairs leading from the first to the second floor were now unaccountably taken down every evening at sunset, by means of a rope and pulleys, and a sentinel, musket in hand, stood under the opening, with a lighted candle near him, ready to prevent any movement on our part in that direction. An order was read to us from Major Turner to the effect that any prisoner approaching the windows, would do so at the peril of his life; the sentries having received strict orders to shoot any one who should touch the prison bars. It was rumored among us that some of the prisoners had written an anonymous communication to Major Turner, informing him that unless he became more lenient in his treatment of us they would " cut his throat," and, as it was quite natural that the young commandant should object to this unpleasant process, it was surmised that all these precautions were taken with a view to its prevention.

But when we learned, through some of the negroes who swept the prison, that General Kilpatrick, with a brigade of cavalry, was within a few miles of Richmond, the true cause of these startling preventive measures was at once apparent to us. It was no doubt feared that we would make an effort to break out, overpower the guards, and endeavor to reach the Federal forces.

On the night of the 3d, we could distinctly hear the cannonading which was going on near the Chickahominy. This would have been exciting enough under any circumstances, but our anxiety was not a little heightened by the well-authenticated information that the cellars of the prison had been mined, and that it was the desperate determination of Major Turner to blow us up sooner than allow us to be liberated by Kilpatrick's raiders. Many were at first skeptical with regard to this barbarous gunpowder-plot, but so positive was the evidence in support of its truth, that the conviction of its reality soon became general. If any skeptics remained, their doubts must have been removed by the statements published in the Richmond papers, to the effect that measures "not necessary to mention at present," had been taken by Major Turner to thwart the proposed liberation of the officers in the Libby, by General Kilpatrick, in case of his capturing the capital. Indeed, some of the prison officials, after the retreat of the raiders, made no secret of it.

With that sort of philosophical nonchalance so sure to be acquired during a long captivity, we laughed at Major Turner's gunpowder plot, and many jokes were enjoyed at the expense of this modern Guy Fawkes. To be sure, with General Kilpatrick thundering away at the fortifications of Richmond, and with the rumored two hundred pounds of gunpowder under our feet, our feelings on the night referred to, were not of the most enviable character. Some of the more nervous, felt quite ill at ease, and some one, as I sat up in my blankets listening to the cannonading, whispered tremblingly in my ear, that he had it from the very best authority, that a soldier was sent down to where the kegs of powder were buried, regularly every half hour during the night, *with a lighted candle*, to see that the fuse was all right!

On the 4th, the body of that gallant soldier, Colonel Dahlgren, was brought into the city.

To-day the rumor is that General Kilpatrick has retired. The rebels are of course jubilant over the escape of their capital from the danger which threatened it. The newspapers are very bitter in their denunciations against the raiders. They say that Colonel Dahlgren's body should have been gibbetted upon the very spot where it was found,—that the prisoners taken from General Kilpatrick's command ought to be immediately hung,—and that if the Confederate capital had been captured, it would have been the signal for the raising of the black flag in every State of the Confederacy.

Peace reigns once more in the prison. The excitement consequent upon General Kilpatrick's raid has died out among us.

There are now rumors, instead, of our being released in what the Rebel authorities would call a *legitimate* way; by which I suppose them to mean that we are to get out of the prison through the door instead of through the *roof*.

The shooting at prisoners at the windows still continues. The sentinels seem to consider it very fine sport, especially those of their number who, never having been at the front, are now afforded an opportunity of displaying their boasted chivalry—with the most perfect safety to themselves. We can see these gallant fellows, with their cocked muskets in their hands, stealthily walking their beats, and glancing wistfully up at our windows in the hope of "getting a shot," as if they were only festive sportsmen, and we but so many squirrels.

Now and then the report of a gun proves that these vigilant sportsmen are not idle. But a few hours ago, one of them was guilty of the most cowardly and cold-blooded attempt at assassination which can be conceived of. Lieut. Hammond, a cavalry officer, one of our number, was standing in one of the boarded enclosures used as a sink, when he was fired at from the pavement below by a dastardly coward in the shape of a Rebel sentinel. The ball grazed Lieut. Hammond's cheek, cut a piece out of his ear, and pierced the rim of his hat. There had been no violation of orders on the prisoner's part—there was no window there—he was not even looking out. The scoundrel who fired at him had been overheard by some of the prisoners to say that he was "bound to shoot one of those d—d Yankees" before he left his beat.

We learned afterwards that the sentinel had been put under arrest.

There is great joy in the prison. We have just heard that forty-eight of our number are to be sent to City Point to-morrow on our way to the North. Those whose confidence in the ability of Major-General Butler to effect an exchange had remained unshaken, have not been disappointed. *Who are to go?* This is the question on the lips of every one.

There are moments in our lives the recollection of which possesses all the unsubstantial qualities of a dream.

The first days of liberation after a protracted captivity are veiled in the misty atmosphere of unreality.

I hear around me the convivial jingling of glasses, the unnatural laughter of familiar prison voices; before me on a spotless table-cloth are an odorous sirloin steak, and a glittering decanter of sherry.

Am I to awake presently, and find myself in my blankets on the cold, hard floor of the Libby, with a bayonet over my head and a voice shouting in harsh Confederate accents: "Get up, here, for roll-call!"

Am I really at "Murphy's"—in Annapolis—under the shadow of the glorious old flag?

Even so—it *must* be true. There is no wild phantasy about this redolent steak—this wine is palpable and warming—there is the unmistakable ring of liberty about the mirthful voices around me.

The happy voyage down the James river to City Point—the first glimpse for so many long, weary months, of the dear old flag flying from the truce boat—the loud cheers for it—the comfortable cabin, made more delightful for us by the courteous *empressement* of Major Mulford, and the cordial sympathy of good Miss Dix—the hearty rounds of cheers from the blockading squadron—Old Point Comfort and Point Lookout—our glorious trip up Chesapeake Bay—our stepping once more upon loyal soil—a delicious bath—clean, new clothing—the sense of regained freedom—an appetizing dinner at genial-hearted Murphy's—all these, pass like the vapory shadows of a vision through my brain, which whirls and reels with delight (it is *not* the wine) as I begin at last to be convinced that I am not dreaming, but that I am once more substantially and positively— FREE!

APPENDIX.

APPENDIX.

Some twenty deaths occurred, of officers confined in the Libby, from July, 1863, to March of the present year. Among them that of the lamented Major Robert Morris, of the 6th Pennsylvania Cavalry, (Rush's Lancers,) who had been a sufferer from scurvy, produced by the quality of the rations upon which he was compelled to subsist in the prison.

Since this narrative was completed, Captain (now Major) H. W. Sawyer, 1st New Jersey Cavalry, and Captain Flinn, sentenced to be hung in retaliation for the execution of Rebel officers in the West, and long held as hostages in the Libby Prison, have been liberated.

BELLE ISLE.

BENJAMIN SWEARER, Color-Sergeant of the 9th Maryland, was among those paroled on the 7th of March, and came North with us on the truce-boat "City of New York." No sooner had he been transferred to the Union steamer than he unwrapped from around his body an American flag, which, with three hearty cheers, was hung up in the cabin. This was the regimental flag of the 9th Maryland. On the 18th of last October, the Rebel Imboden attacked Colonel Simpson's regiment, then doing duty at Charlestown, Va., and among the captured was Sergeant Swearer. This brave man had torn one of the flags from the lance and had concealed it around his body; the other flag he refused to surrender, although threatened with instant death by his captors, and tore it into shreds before their eyes. During more than four months he had been a prisoner on Belle Isle, and had succeeded in concealing this flag, although frequent searches were made for it by the Rebel officials, who had reason to suspect that Swearer had brought it with him. Upon our arrival at Annapolis the cherished flag was attached to a lance, and the gallant Color-Sergeant stepped once again upon loyal soil under the shadow of that banner he had sworn never to forsake, and which, defended and shielded on the battle-field and in the prison, he now bore proudly back, unpolluted by Rebel hands, to his comrades.

APPENDIX.

LIBBY PRISON, RICHMOND, VA.,
December 29, 1863.

LIEUTENANT-COLONEL CAVADA having drawn numerous sketches illustrative of our life in this prison, and having collected many interesting notes in connection with the same, we, the undersigned, respectfully request him to have them published, in book form, as soon as possible after his liberation.

Brigadier-General Neal Dow, . United States Volunteers.
Colonel Chas. W. Tilden, . . 16th Maine Volunteers.
" Louis de Cesnola, . . 4th New York Cavalry.
Lieutenant Thos. Morley, . . 12th Pennsylvania Volunteers.
Captain E. Charlier, . .
" E. W. Atwood, . . 16th Maine Volunteers.
Lieutenant Butler Coles, . .
" D. P. Rennie, . .
W. E. H. Fentress, . . . United States Navy.
Captain Wm. C. Wilson, . .
Lieutenant Wm. Nice, . .
M. C. Wadsworth, . . .
Lieutenant J. Arthur Richardson,
" Mason Gray, . .
" George A. Chandler, .
Captain Charles Hasty, . .
Captain E. Szabad, . . . General French's Staff.
Lieutenant Geo. C. Houston, .
Major Samuel McIrvin, . . 1st New York Cavalry.
Captain Fred'k Barton, . .
" Francis Irch, . . 45th New York Volunteers.
Lieutenant Henry Alert, . . " " "
Captain Jas. W. Vanderhoff, . " " "
Lieutenant Hugo Chandler, . " " "
Captain Wm. Spring, . . . " " "

Lieutenant T. Leydhecker,	45th New York Volunteers.
" Edward Kunckel,	" " "
Captain Jno. Hell,	" " "
" Henry Deitz,	" " "
Lieutenant Henry Bath,	" " "
" Louis Lindemeyer,	" " "
" George Schule,	" " "
" Adam Hanf,	" " "
Lieutenant-Colonel Adolf Haack,	68th " "
Lieutenant Otto Gerson,	45th " "
Adjutant C. L. Alstaedt,	54th " "
Captain Otto Mussehl,	68th " "
" W. Domnchke,	
Major S. Roovacs,	
Adjutant Albert Walber,	26th Wisconsin Volunteers.
Lieutenant George M. Brush,	
" S. S. Stearns,	4th Maine Volunteers.
" Victor Mylius,	
Major Alex. Von Mitzel,	
Captain Oscar Templeton,	
" James A. Carman,	
Lieutenant Eugene Hepp,	
Lieutenant J. F. Newbrandt,	4th Missouri Cavalry.
" Geo. L. Garrett,	" "
" Jno. Q. Carpenter,	
Captain H. W. Sawyer,	1st New Jersey Cavalry.
Lieutenant James U. Childs,	16th Maine Volunteers.
Adjutant O. Owen Jones,	2d New York Cavalry.
Lieutenant Thomas Huggins,	2d New York Volunteers.
" C. J. Davis,	1st Massachusetts Cavalry.
Major H. A. White,	13th Pennsylvania Cavalry.
Lieutenant Jno. D. Simpson,	10th Indiana Volunteers.
" Yeat Bickham,	19th United States Infantry.
" M. M. Moore,	6th Michigan Cavalry.
" Morton Tower,	13th Massachusetts Volunteers.
" Joseph Chatburn,	150th Pennsylvania Volunteers.
" H. B. Seeley,	86th New York Volunteers.
" Jno. McGovern,	73d Pennsylvania Volunteers.

APPENDIX. 207

A. D. Renshaw,	United States Navy.
James McCaulley	" "
Lieutenant Harry E. Rulon,	114th Pennsylvania Volunteers.
" Edward P. Brooks,	16th Wisconsin Volunteers.
Captain Geo. G. Davis,	4th Maine Volunteers.
" M. R. Baldwin.	2d Wisconsin Volunteers.
Lieutenant A. W. Sprague,	24th Michigan Volunteers.
" H. A. Curtice,	157th New York Volunteers.
Captain P. H. Hart,	19th Indiana Volunteers.
Lieutenant D. J. Connolly,	63d New York Volunteers.
" C. H. Drake,	142d Pennsylvania Volunteers.
Captain E. C. Alexander,	1st Delaware Volunteers.
Lieutenant J. Harl'd Richardson,	19th Indiana Volunteers.
" W. H. H. Wilcox,	10th New York Volunteers.
Lieutenant Nathan A. Robbins,	4th Maine Volunteers.
" E. L. Palmer,	57th New York Volunteers.
Major Wm. D. Morton,	14th New York Cavalry.
Adjutant George H. Gamble,	8th Illinois Cavalry.
Lieutenant Joseph H. Potts,	75th Ohio Volunteers.
" George R. Barce,	5th Michigan Cavalry.
" Wm Nelson,	United States Infantry.
" G. Veltfort,	54th New York Volunteers.
Adjutant Jno. Sullivan,	7th Rhode Island Volunteers.
Lieutenant H. A. Hubbard,	12th New York Cavalry.
" A. W. Locklin,	94th New York Volunteers.
" H. E. Mosher,	12th New York Cavalry.
Captain C. C. Comer,	94th New York Volunteers.
Lieutenant E. Chas. Parker,	" " "
" D. E. Sears,	" " "
" Jno. Ryan,	69th Pennsylvania Volunteers.
Captain Edmund H. Mass,	88th " "
Lieutenant Hyde Crocker,	1st New Jersey Cavalry.
Captain Wm. K Boltz,	
Lieutenant T. Paulding,	6th United States Cavalry.
" Freeman C. Gay,	11th Pennsylvania Volunteers.
" T. J. Crosley,	57th " "
" Fuller Dingley,	7th Rhode Island Volunteers.
Captain J. M. Dushane,	

15

Major Frank Place,	157th New York Volunteers.
Lieutenant Thos. J. Dean,	5th Michigan Cavalry.
Captain Emile Frey,	82d Illinois Volunteers.
Lieutenant Hugo Gerhardt,	24th " "
Lieutenant Chas. Fritze,	24th Illinois Volunteers.
Wm. Kruger,	2d Missouri Volunteers.
Lieutenant Fred'k Schweinforth,	
Captain Robert H. Day,	56th Pennsylvania Volunteers.
" Wm. B. Avery,	132d New York Volunteers.
Lieutenant Thos. Meyers,	107 Pennsylvania Volunteers.
" S. R Colladay,	6th Pennsylvania Cavalry.
" Welcome Fenner,	2d Rhode Island Cavalry.
Captain Alfred Heffley,	142d Pennsylvania Volunteers.
Wm. H. Fogg,	United States Navy.
Adjutant Jno A. Garcis.	1st Maryland Cavalry.
Lieutenant Henry Apple,	" " "
" Leopold Meyer,	
" Gustave Hellenberg,	1st Rhode Island Volunteers.
Captain David Schortz.	12th Pennsylvania Cavalry.
Lieutenant W. W. Paxton,	140th Pennsylvania Volunteers.
Major Jno. E. Clark.	
Lieutenant Henry H Hinds,	57th " "
" H. V. Knight,	20th Michigan Volunteers.
Captain S. A Urquhart,	
Lieutenant S. H. Ballard,	5th Michigan Cavalry.
Captain C. C. Widdis,	150th Pennsylvania Volunteers.
Lieutenant D. W. Hakes,	18th Connecticut Volunteers.
Major Chas. Farnsworth.	1st Connecticut Cavalry.
Major W. N. Denny,	
Lieutenant Eugene H. Fales,	
" J. Bedwell,	
" Morgan Kupp,	167th Pennsylvania Volunteers.
Colonel W. H. Powell.	
Lieutenant Henry S. Platt.	
Captain Charles E. Rowan,	
" Matt Boyd,	
" Wm. M. Kendall,	
Lieutenant H. H. Tillotson,	

APPENDIX.

Captain David Getman,
" Eberhart,
Lieutenant E. J. Spaulding,
Colonel A. H. Tippen, . . . 58th Pennsylvania Volunteers.
L. S Stone,
Lieutenant Will. Blanchard, . 2d United States Cavalry.
" Andrew Stoll, . . 6th "   "
John Halderman,
Lieutenant Jeff Weakley,
" R. J. Connolly,
Captain Wm. Wallick,
Lieutenant James Adams,
" James C. Woodrow,
" Jno. Bradford,
Captain Wm. R. Wright,
Lieutenant S. S. Holbrook,
Captain James M. Imbrie,
" Wm. F. Martins,
Lieutenant H. Reece Whiting,
Captain Chas. B ron,
Lieutenant John Ritchie,
Captain J. H. Whelan,
Wm. H. A. Forsyth,
Lieutenant J. W. Mundy,
" B. F. Henington,
Colonel F. Bartleson,
Lieutenant H. P. Freeman,
" J. H. Gageby,
Colonel W. P. Kindrick,
Lieutenant Rich'd H. Pond, . 12th U. S. Infantry.
Captain W. C. Rossman,
Lieutenant Samuel T. C Mervin,
" Judson S. Paul,
" John Sweadner,
Colonel Wm B. McCreery,
Lieutenant H. S. Bevington,
Captain David Hay,
" Geo H. Starr,

Lieutenant Chas. H Livingston, .
" Frank A. Hubbell, .
" Mendes C. Bryant, .
" Stephen D. Carpenter,
" John W. McComas, .
" Wm. J. Morris, . .
Captain Geo. C. Gordon, . .
" J. W. Chamberlain, .
Lieutenant Wm. L. Watson, .
" N. L. Wood, Jr., .
" L. N. Duchesney, .
" Wm. A Dailey, . .
" James H. Kellogg, .
" Wm. Bierbower, . 87th Pensylvania Volunteers
Captain Nath. Rollins, . .
" Thos. Reed, . . .
Mr. George Reed, . . .
Captain G. M. White, . . .
Lieutenant H. C. Smith, . .
Captain John Bird, . . .
Lieutenant S. P. Gamble, . . 57th Pennsylvania Volunteers.
" Wallace F. Randolph, 5th United States Artillery.
Major E. M. Pope, . .
Lieutenant G. S. Goal, . .
Captain M. Gallagher, . . .
" John Kennedy, . . 73d Pennsylvania Volunteers.
" Kin. S. Dygert, . .
Lieutenant Samuel G. Boone, . 88th Pennsylvania Volunteers.
" George W. Grant, . " " "
Lieut.-Colonel Ivan N. Walker, .
Lieutenant James F. Pool, . .
" James Kane, . .
" Geo. W. Chandler, .
" Joseph P. Rockwell, .
" J. A. Delano, . .
" Wm. Oakley Butler, .
Colonel William G. Ely, . . 18th Connecticut Volunteers.
Lieutenant J. Paul Jones, . . 55th Ohio Volunteers.

APPENDIX. 211

Lieutenant Lewis R. Titus, . .
" John Davidson, . .
" H. B. Kelly, . . 6th Kentucky Cavalry.
" Rufus F. Thorne, .
Captain John W. Lewis, . . 4th Kentucky Cavalry.
" S. D. Conover, . .
Lieutenant George Maw, . . 86th Ohio.
" J. N. Whitney, . .
Captain B. G. Caster, . .
Lieutenant James Hersch, . .
Charles W. Earle, . . .
Lieutenant J. S. Powers, . .
T. W. Boyce, ...
Captain John Teed, . . . 116th Pennsylvania Volunteers.
Lieutenant W. B. Clark, . .
" Thompson Lennig, . 6th Pennsylvania Cavalry.
Thomas Brown, ... United States Navy.
Captain A. J. Makepiece, . .
Lieutenant L. P. Williams, . .
" George H. Morisey, .
Lieut.-Colonel R. S. Northcott, .
" Jno. W. Kennedy. .
" Chas. W. Drake, .
" M. V. B. Morrison, .
Riley Johnson, ...
Edward Potter, ...
Captain Daniel F. Kelly, . . 73d Pennsylvania Volunteers.
" John Kelly, . . " " "
Lieutenant Samuel Irvin, . .
" John W. Austin, .
" Michael Hoffman, .
" Adam Dixon, . .
Captain Henry C. Davis, . .
Lieutenant Thomas H. McKee, .
J B. Sampson, ...
A. W. Loomis, ...
E. B. Bascom, ...
Cyrus P. Heffley, ...

S. H. M. Byers, ...
Lieutenant Byron Davis, . . 72d Pennsylvania Volunteers.
Lieutenant A. Wilson Norris, . 107th Pennsylvania Volunteers.
Sidney Meade, ...
Lieutenant William W. Calkins, .
" C. W. Catlett, . .
Captain William M. Murry, .
" Weston Rouand, . . 1st Virginia Cavalry.
Lieutenant Charles P. Potts, . 151st Pennsylvania Volunteers.
" William Heffner, .
Captain Leonard B. Blinn, . .
William L. Brown, . . .
Captain James T. Morgan, . .
Lieutenant William H. Crawford,
" H. F. Meyer, . .
" D. O. Kelly, . . 100th Ohio Volunteers.
William A. Worl, . . . 5th Indiana Volunteers.
Major N. S. Marshall, . . 5th Iowa Volunteers.
Captain J. C. Rollins, . . 8th Tennessee Cavalry.
" E. J. Mathewson, . . 18th Connecticut Volunteers.
Lieutenant H. H. Mosely, . . 25th Ohio Volunteers.
Adjutant William S. Marshall, . 51st Indiana Volunteers.
Lieutenant Henry F. Cowles, . . 18th Connecticut Volunteers.
Adjutant Guy Bryan, . . . 8th Pennsylvania Volunteers.
Captain William L. Gray, . . 151st Pennsylvania Volunteers.
Lieutenant John H. Stevens, . 5th Maine.
Thomas C. Wentworth, . .
Captain L. C. Bisbee, . . .
" F. M. Shoemaker, . . 100th Ohio Volunteers.
Charles G. Peterson, . . .
Lieutenant David Whiston, . . 13th Massachusetts Volunteers.
" Samuel E. Cary, . " " "
Lieutenant George Halpin, . . 116th Pennsylvania Volunteers.
" Horace Gamble, . 73d Indiana Volunteers.
Lieut.-Colonel Jere. Williams, .
Captain J. E. Woodward, . .
Lieutenant Israel N. Kibbee, .
Adam H. Lindsay, . . .

Captain James A. Penfield, . 5th New York Cavalry.
" S. B. Ryder, . . . " "
" William D. Lucas, . . " "
Francis McKeag, ...
M. V. B. Tiffany, ...
Captain E. A. Sheppard, . .
" J. G. Weld, . . .
" J. B. Fay, . . .
" Edward Porter, . . 154th New York Volunteers.
Lieutenant C. G. Stevens, . . " " "
Captain J. Riley Stone, . .
Lieutenant Theo. Kendall, . .
John W. Right, ...
Lieutenant J. O. Rockwell, .
Samuel H. Erving, . . .
James H. Cain, ...
Lieutenant Frank Moran, . .
" James Heslet, . .
Samuel H. Treasonthick, . .
Captain J. D. Phelps, . . .
" Adolph Kuhn, . .
John L. Brown, ...
Lieutenant Lewis Thompson, . 5th United States Cavalry.
Major W. B. Neeper, . . . 57th Pennsylvania Volunteers.
Lieutenant G. A. Potter, . .
Captain Jno. A. Arthur, . .
" Jno. Craig, . . . 1st Virginia Volunteers.
Lieutenant Edwd. E. Andrews, .
Captain J. P. Cummins, . . 9th Maryland Volunteers.
Lieutenant R. Gates, . . . 18th United States Infantry.
" Jerry Mooney, . . 107th Pennsylvania Volunteers.
J. W. Steele, ...
Lieutenant William G. Purnell, . 5th Maryland Volunteers.
Captain R. O. Ives, . . . 10th Massachusetts Volunteers.
Lieut.-Colonel C. H. Morton, . .
Major J. R. Muhleman, . .
Lieutenant Ed. Knoble, . .
" David Garbit, . .

Major Alex. Phillips,	77th Pennsylvania Volunteers.
Captain William A. Collins,	
Lieutenant John W. Worth,	5th Maryland Volunteers.
Major J. P. Collins,	29th Indiana Volunteers.
Captain T. Clark,	79th Illinois Volunteers.
Lieutenant George Harris,	" " "
" Lester D. Phelps,	8th Pennsylvania Cavalry.
" Otho P. Fairfield,	
Captain William A. Robinson,	
" William L. Hubbell,	17th Connecticut Volunteers.
" Milton Russell,	
Lieutenant William A. Adair	
" J. D. Higgins,	
Captain John Birch,	
" Jno. A. Scammahorn,	
Lieutenant Martin Flick	
" W. Wilson,	
" M. Fellows,	149th Pennsylvania Volunteers.
Isaac Johnson,	United States Navy.
Captain C. H. Riggs,	123d Ohio Volunteers.
Lieutenant Harry Wilson,	18th Pennsylvania Cavalry.
" Fred. J. Brownell,	
" William H. Harvey,	
Captain Jno. F. Randolph,	
Lieut.-Col. Gustav Von Helmrich.	4th Missouri Cavalry.
Captain Newton C. Pace,	
Major E. N. Bates,	
Lieut.-Colonel A. F. Rodgers.	
" Ezra D. Carpenter,	
Adjutant Charles N. Winner,	1st Ohio Volunteers.
Lieutenant Charles M. Gross,	110th Ohio Volunteers.
Major Josiah Hall,	1st Vermont Cavalry.
Captain E. Dillingham,	" "
" William N. Beeman,	" "
Lieutenant Lewis C. Mead,	22d Michigan Volunteers.
Captain William H. Bender,	123d Ohio Volunteers.
Lieutenant Jacob S. Devine,	71st Pennsylvania Volunteers.
" J. Riley Weaver,	18th Pennsylvania Cavalry.

APPENDIX.

Adjutant A. S. Mathews,	22d Michigan Volunteers.
Captain A. W. Keeler,	" " "
" E. M. Driscoll,	3d Ohio Volunteers.
Lieutenant John C. Roney,	" "
" George W. Fish.	" "
Lieutenant F. B. Stevenson,	3d Ohio Volunteers.
" James H. Murdock,	" "
" E. E. Sharp,	51st Indiana Volunteers.
" C. L. Irwin,	78th Illinois Volunteers.
" Charles Trownsell,	8th Ohio Volunteers.
" David S. Bartram,	18th Connecticut Volunteers.
" A. K. Dunkle,	114th Pennsylvania Volunteers.
" Geo. L. Snyder,	104th New York Volunteers.
Captain James A. Coffin,	157th New York Volunteers.
" H. C. McQuiddy,	73d Pennsylvania Volunteers.
Lieutenant A. A. Taylor,	122d Ohio Volunteers.
" Frank A. M. Kreps,	77th Pennsylvania Volunteers.
" Geo. L. Sollers,	9th Indiana Volunteers.
Lieut.-Colonel J. P. Spofford,	97th New York Volunteers.
Captain John McMahon,	94th New York Volunteers.
" Solomon G. Hamlin,	134th New York Volunteers.
Edward L. Haines,	United States Navy.
Captain John G. Whiteside,	94th New York Volunteers.
Lieutenant Edwin Tuthill,	104th New York Volunteers.
" Thomas W. Johnston,	10th New York Cavalry.
" James J. Higginson,	
Captain H. G. White,	94th New York Volunteers.
Lieutenant J. H. Russell.	12th Massachusetts Volunteers.
" William T. Wheeler,	
" Isaac Ludlow,	3d United States Artillery.
P. H. White,	
Lieutenant J. T. Maginnis,	18th Connecticut Volunteers.
Adjutant R. C. Knaggs,	
V. R. Davis,	
R. W. Anderson,	
Captain John B. McRoberts,	
Robert H. Montgomery,	
Captain John E. Page,	

Lieutenant J. L. Powers, . . 157th New York Volunteers.
Lieut.-Colonel S. M. Archer, . 17th Iowa Volunteers.
    " H. M. Anderson, .
Captain S. O. Pool, . . 154th New York Volunteers.
    " J. R. Day, . . 3d Maine Volunteers.
    " V. K. Hart, . . 19th United States Infantry.
Lieutenant William Nelson, . 13th United States Infantry.
Captain W. W. Hunt, . . 100th Ohio Volunteers.
    " W. W. Scearce, .
Lieut.-Colonel D. A. McHolland, 51st Indiana Volunteers.
    " John Egen, . . 69th Pennsylvania Volunteers.
Major G. M. Van Buren, . . 6th New York Cavalry.
Lieutenant Thos. S. Armstrong, . 122d Ohio Volunteers.
Captain Sidney B. King, . . 12th Pennsylvania Cavalry.
Lieutenant Harry Temple, . . 2d New York Cavalry.
Captain Edward. P. Boas, . . 20th Illinois Volunteers.
Lieutenant Charles D. Henry, . 4th Ohio Volunteers.
Captain John Cutter, . . 34th Ohio Volunteers.
Captain J. A. Rufield, . . 5th New York Cavalry.
    " James F. Jennings, . 45th Ohio Volunteers.
    " Adam R. Eglin, . . " " "
    " Geo. W. Greene, . . 19th Indiana Volunteers.
Lieutenant Jos. Wilshire, .
    " J. Gilbert Blue, . . 3d Ohio Volunteers.
Captain Geo. L. Schell, . . 88th Pennsylvania Volunteers.
    " James Galt, . .
    " Benj. F. Campbell, . 36th Illinois Volunteers.
Lieutenant John A. Francis, . 18th Connecticut Volunteers.
    " C. W. Pavey, . . 80th Illinois Volunteers.
Captain Edward A. Tobes, .
    " George R. Lodge, . . 53d Illinois Volunteers.
Lieutenant Alfred Gude, . . 51st Indiana Volunteers.
Captain Willington Willits, . 7th Michigan Cavalry.
    " William H. Smyth, . 16th United States Infantry.
Lieutenant John T. Mackey, . " " " "
    " John C. Norcross, . 2d Massachusetts Cavalry.
    " Jerry Keniston, . . 100th Illinois Infantry.
    " Samuel Koach, . . " " "

APPENDIX. 217

Lieutenant F. A. Lakin, . . 18th Indiana Volunteers.
Captain W. F. Pickerill, . . 5th Iowa Infantry.
Lieut.-Colonel A. P. Henry, .
Major W. N. Owens, . . .
Captain D. L. Wright, . . .
    " Horace Noble, . .
Lieutenant Alexander H. White,
    " C. L. Anderson, . .
    " E. McBaron Timoney, 15th United States Infantry.
    " M. Morris, . . . 93d Illinois Infantry.
Lieutenant Stiles H. Boughton, .
    " James McKinley, .
    " M. Cohen, . . .
    " R. Curtis, . . . 4th Kentucky Cavalry.
    " Ara C. Spofford, . 21st Ohio Volunteers.
    " John V. Patterson, .
    " Edgar J. Higby, . 33d Ohio Volunteers.
Adjutant John W. Thomas, . 2d Ohio Volunteers.
Lieutenant Martin V. Dickey, . 2d Ohio Volunteer Infantry.
Captain D. W. Olcott, . . 134th New York Volunteers.
Lieutenant A. J. Teeter, . . 2d Ohio Volunteer Infantry.
    " W. B. Cook, . . 140th Pennsylvania Volunteers.
Captain George A. Crocker, . 6th New York Cavalry.
    " Frank R. Josselyn, . 11th Massachusetts Volunteers.
    " Jacob Remie, . .   "   "   "
    " Samuel E. Cary, .
Adjutant James Gilmore, . . 79th New York Volunteers.
Lieutenant Joseph Kerrin, . . 6th United States Cavalry.
    " B. H. Herkness, . 6th Pennsylvania Cavalry.
    " F. Harry Stewart, . 5th Maryland Volunteers.
    " L. S. Smith, . . 14th New York Cavalay.
    " John King, . . 15th Illinois Cavalry.
    " Frank T. Bennett, . 18th United States Infantry.
Captain W. H. Douglass, . .
    " John Carrol, . . .
    " Fred. Nemmert, . .
    " A. H. Wonder, . . 51st Indiana Volunteers.
Lieutenant Thomas G. Good, . 1st Maryland Cavalry.

Lieutenant Thomas B. Dewees,	2d United States Cavalry.
" H. Moulton,	1st " " "
" Thomas A. Worthen,	118th Illinois Volunteers.
Captain G. C. Urwiler,	67th Pennsylvania Volunteers.
Lieutenant A. K. Wolback,	3d Ohio Volunteers.
Captain Henry Hescock,	1st Missouri Artillery.
John S. Manning,	
Lieutenant David R. Lock,	8th Kentucky Cavalry.
Captain W. F. Conrad,	25th Iowa Volunteers.
Lieutenant D. C. Dillon,	7th Iowa Volunteers.
" John S. Mahoney,	21st Ohio Volunteers.
Lieut.-Colonel Monroe Nichols,	18th Connecticut Volunteers.
Lieutenant George Rings,	100th Ohio Volunteers.
Major A. McMahan,	21st Ohio Volunteers.
Lieutenant M. V. B. Callahan,	
Captain D. D. Smith,	1st Alabama Cavalry.
Lieutenant E. J. Davis,	44th Illinois Volunteers.
" Joseph Smith,	67th Pennsylvania Volunteers.
" Emory W. Pelton,	2d Maryland Volunteers.
" W. A. Merry,	106th New York Volunteers.
" C. Poller Stroman,	87th Pennsylvania Volunteers.
Captain Bryant Grafton,	64th Ohio Volunteers.
Lieutenant T. Fowler,	67th Pennsylvania Volunteers.
Adjutant L. W. Sutherland,	126th Ohio Volunteers.
Lieutenant A. G. Griffin,	112th Illinois Volunteers.
Captain J. E. Wilkins,	" " "
Robert T. Fisher,	
Colonel W. T. Wilson,	123d Ohio Volunteers.
Lieutenant B. F. Blair,	" "
Captain J. C. Hagenbush,	67th Pennsylvania Volunteers.
Lieutenant R. O. Knowles,	116th Ohio Volunteers.
" C. E. Harrison,	89th Ohio Volunteers.
" J. R. Mell,	51st Ohio Volunteers.
" Z. R. Prather,	116th Illinois Volunteers.
G. W. Moore,	
Lieutenant W. L. Ritilly,	51st Ohio Volunteers.
Captain J. W. Fasler,	42d Illinois Volunteers.
Lieutenant M. C. Causten,	19th United States Infantry.

APPENDIX. 219

Lieut.-Colonel H. B. Hunter,	123 Ohio Volunteers.
Major T. B. Rogers,	140th Pennsylvania Volunteers.
Lieutenant George H. Morrisey,	12th Iowa Volunteers.
Captain P. H. Hart,	19th Indiana Volunteers.
Lieutenant D. C. Dillon,	7th Iowa Volunteers.
Captain G. M. White,	1st Virginia Volunteers.
Lieutenant G. W. Hale,	101st Ohio Volunteers.
" Hanson P. Jordan,	9th Indiana Volunteers.
" George F. Robinson,	80th Ohio Volunteers.
" W. J. M. Connelee,	4th Iowa Volunteers.
" Andrew Stoll,	7th United States Cavalry.
" P. Hagan,	7th Maryland Volunteers.
" G. B. Coleman,	6th United States Vol. Cavalry.
" M. H. Smith,	123d Ohio Volunteers.
Captain D. H. Mull,	
Lieutenant A. N. Thomas,	
Captain W. M. Cockrum,	42d Indiana Volunteers.
Lieutenant F. B. Colver,	123d Ohio Volunteers.
" Isaac Hull,	
" DeFontaine,	73d Pennsylvania Volunteers.
" F. L. Schyler,	123d Ohio Volunteers.
" S. Leith,	132d New York Volunteers.
" A. W. Locklin,	94th New York Volunteers.
" H. H. Hinds,	57th Pennsylvania Volunteers.
Captain John F. Porter, Jr.,	14th N. Y. Cavalry.
" John A. Russell,	93d Illinois Volunteers.
" John C. Shroed,	
Lieutenant James Carothers,	78th Ohio Volunteers.
Ensign Simon H. Strunk,	United States Navy.
Lieutenant W. H. McDill,	
" A. G. Scranton,	
Lieut.-Colonel R. Von Schrader,	
Irenus McGowan,	
Lieutenant Thomas W. Boyce,	
" R. J. Harmer,	
" Louis R. Fortescue,	
" J. L. Leslie,	18th Pennsylvania Cavalry.
Captain O. H. Rosenbaum,	123d Ohio Volunteers.

Lieutenant William Willis,	51st Indiana Volunteers.
Captain William A. Swayze,	3d Ohio Volunteers.
Lieutenant O. P. Barnes,	3d Ohio Volunteer Infantry.
" A. M. Stark,	Q. M. 110th Ohio Volunteer Inf.
Adjutant S. B. Piper,	3d Ohio Volunteer Infantry.
Captain H. P. Wands,	22d Michigan Volunteers.
" J. Marche McComas,	9th Missouri Volunteers.
Lieutenant Lewis Drake,	22d Michigan Volunteers.
Captain J. DeWitt Whiting,	3d Ohio Volunteers.
Lieutenant W. A. Curry,	3d Ohio Volunteer Infantry.
Captain John C. Johnson,	149th Pennsylvania Volunteers.
Lieutenant Gideon T. Hand,	51st Indiana Volunteers.
" Charles F. Barclay,	149th Pennsylvania Volunteers.
Adjutant Melville R. Small,	6th Maryland Cavalry.
Lieutenant A. T. Lamson,	104th New York Volunteers.
Adjutant N. McEvoy,	3d Illinois Cavalry.
Lieutenant H. C. Potter,	18th Pennsylvania Cavalry.
Captain H. C. White,	94th New York Volunteers.
Lieutenant Francis Murphy,	97th New York Volunteers.
Captain Milton Ewing,	21st Wisconsin Volunteers.
Lieutenant Henry C. Taylor,	21st Wisconsin Volunteers.
Captain George W. Warner,	18th Connecticut Volunteers.
Colonel Heber LeFavour,	22d Michigan Volunteers.
Lieutenant Henry T. Anschutz,	12th Virginia Volunteers.
Lieut.-Col. James H. Wing,	3d Ohio Volunteer Infantry.
Major B. B. McDonald,	101st Ohio Volunteer Infantry.
Lieutenant John Sterling,	30th Indiana Volunteers.
Captain A. G. Hamilton,	12th Kentucky Cavalry.
" McCaslin Moore,	29th Indiana Volunteers.
Lieutenant Eli Foster,	30th Indiana Volunteers.
Lieut.-Colonel David Miles,	79th Pennsylvania Volunteers.
Captain A. J. Bigelow,	79th Illinois Volunteers.
" John F. Gallagher,	2d Ohio Volunteer Infantry.
Lieutenant Thos. G. Cochran,	77th Pennsylvania Volunteers.
Captain Thomas Handy,	79th Illinois Volunteers.
Lieutenant E. C. Gordon,	
" Alfred S. Cooper,	9th Indiana Volunteers.
" G. D. Bisbee,	16th Maine Volunteers.

APPENDIX.

Lieutenant Abraham Allee,	16th Illinois Cavalry.
E. G. Dayton,	United States Navy.
Lieutenant D. M. V. Stuart,	10th Missouri Infantry.
" H. S. Murdock,	73d Indiana Volunteers.
" G. W. Moore,	
" H. H. Fillotson,	73d Indiana Volunteers.
" C. M. Prutsman,	7th Wisconsin Volunteers.
Captain Samuel McKee,	14th Kentucky Cavalry.
Lieutenant Jos. F. Carter,	9th Maryland Volunteers.
" James Weatherbee,	51st Ohio Volunteers.
" Robert Huey,	2d E. Tennessee Volunteers.
" A. B. Alger,	22d Ohio Volunteers.
Major T. B. Rogers,	140th Pennsylvania Volunteers.
Lieutenant George W. Bulton,	22d Michigan Volunteers.
" William H. Locke,	
Lieutenant M. B. Helms,	1st Virginia Volunteers.
" E. J. Gorgas,	Co. A. 90th Regt. Penn. Vols.
" Ira Tyler,	7th Maryland Volunteers.
Captain F. Irsch,	45th New York Volunteers.
" L. T. Borchiss,	67th Pennsylvania Volunteers.
" G. A. Manning,	2d Massachusetts Cavalry.
" J. W. Whelan,	A. A. G.
Major J. C. Edmonds,	32d Massachusetts Volunteers.
" H. B. Neeper,	57th Pennsylvania Volunteers.
Captain F. B. Doten,	14th Connecticut Volunteers.

The hole in the Floor.

EXPERIENCES OF A PRISONER OF WAR in RICHMOND, Va., 1863–64.

By Lieut-Col. F. F. Cavada, U.S.V.

PHILADELPHIA: KING & BAIRD, No. 607 SANSOM STREET.
1864.

"Five for a Dollar"